Between Positivism and T.S. Eliot:

Imagism and T.E. Hulme

Flemming Olsen

BETWEEN POSITIVISM AND T.S. ELIOT: IMAGISM AND T.E. HULME

UNIVERSITY PRESS OF SOUTHERN DENMARK 2008

University of Southern Denmark
Studies in Literature vol. 52

© Flemming Olsen and University Press of Southern Denmark
Set and printed by Grafisk Data Center A/S, Odense
Cover design by Anne Charlotte Mouret, Side-1
ISBN 978-87-7674-283-6

Printed with support from Landsdommer V. Gieses Legat

University Press of Southern Denmark
Campusvej 55
DK-5230 Odense M
Phone: +45 6615 7999
Fax: +45 6615 8126
Press@forlag.sdu.dk
www.universitypress.dk

Distribution in the United States and Canada:
International Specialized Book Services
5804 NE Hassalo Street
Portland, OR 97213-3644 USA
www.isbs.com

Distribution in the United Kingdom:
Gazelle
White Cross Mills
Hightown
Lancaster
LA1 4 XS
U.K.
www.gazellebooks.co.uk

Syddansk Universitetsforlag
Campusvej 55
5230 Odense M

Tlf. 66 15 79 99
Fax 66 15 81 26

www.universitypress.dk

Table of Contents

PREFACE 9

CHAPTER ONE: IMAGISM
   Name. Origin. Members 11
   A New Note 13
   The World and the Poet 14
   Language 15
   Form 16
   Content 17
   The Imagist Principles 17
   Imagist Criticism of Imagism 19
   Vorticism 21

CHAPTER TWO: THE LATE 19TH CENTURY SCIENTIFIC MODEL
   Introduction 23
   Lord Kelvin 23
   Reality 25

CHAPTER THREE: THE PERVASIVENESS OF THE MODEL
   Ernst Mach 27
   Herbert Spencer 28
   August Comte 30
   Hippolyte Taine 33

CHAPTER FOUR: POSITIVISM AND ITS LIMITATIONS
   Positivism 37
   Limitations 39
   The Scientists 41
   The Philosophers 42

CHAPTER FIVE: COUNTERCURRENTS
   L'art pour l'art 50
   Theodor Lipps 51
   John Ruskin 52
   French Influence 53
   Mimesis 53
   Creation. Ribot 54
   Gourmont 55
   Laforgue 57

CHAPTER SIX: BREAKTHROUGH OF THE ANTI-POSITIVISTS
- Planck 61
- Einstein 62
- The Humanities 62
- Symbolism 64

CHAPTER SEVEN: INDEBTEDNESS
- Introduction 67
- Wittgenstein 67
- Dynamism and Categorization 68
- Bergson 69
- Bergson and Hulme 71
- Form 72
- Worringer 72
- *Vers libre* 74
- Dance 78

CHAPTER EIGHT: HULME'S PHILOSOPHY
- Introduction 81
- Argumentation 82
- Absolutes 83
- Hulme and Science 84
- Bergson 85
- Dichotomies 85
- Intuition versus Intellect 85
- Manifolds 86
- Humanism and Religion 87
- Values 88
- Conclusion 89

CHAPTER NINE: HULME'S AESTHETICS
- Introduction 91
- The Purpose of Art 92
- Dichotomies 93
- Form 93
- Geometric versus Vital Art 93
- Classical versus Romantic 95
- Beauty 96
- Creation 97
- Hulme and Politics 98

CHAPTER TEN: HULME'S LITERARY THEORIES
- Introduction 99
- Science and Poetry 100
- The Poet 101

Literature and its Raw Materials	102
The Creative Process	103
Fancy and Imagination	106
The Subject	106
Mimesis	107
Form	108
Language	111
Cinders and Counters	113
The Function of the Image	117
The Reader	117
The Objective Correlative	118

CHAPTER ELEVEN: HULME'S POEMS

Introduction	123
Themes	124
Composition	127
Form	128
Vocabulary	129
Characters	131
Images	132

CHAPTER TWELVE: HULME CRITICISM 137

CONCLUSION

Positivism	143
Imagism	144
Hulme	145
The Legacy	145
Eliot	146
Later Developments	147
Final Remarks	147

BIBLIOGRAPHY 149

ALPHABETICAL INDEX 163

NOTES 173

Preface

Several critics have been intrigued by the gap between late Victorian poetry and the more "modern" poetry of the 1920s. It is my contention that a close analysis of the poetry and criticism written in the first decade of the 20th century and until the end of the First World War – excluding war poetry – will be rewarding if we want to acquire a greater understanding of the transition.

The book is not meant as a total overview of the intellectual climate in England from Tennyson to Eliot. Rather, it describes the development that took place within art and literature – especially poetry – as a reaction against the positivist attitude. Early in the 19th century, science came to be taken as the opposite of poetry because the Romanticists conceived of the lyrical poem as the outlet of the poet's feelings. That attitude was dominant during the rest of the 19th century.

To many readers and critics, T.E.Hulme represents little more thasn a footnote. He is vaguely known as one of the precursors of the far more interesting T.S.Eliot, for which reason some lip-service may be paid to him, but his own achievement is hardly ever referred to.

Hulme and the Imagists represent an intermediary stage between Tennyson and Eliot, but they are more than mere stepping-stones. Besides being experimenting poets, most of them are acute critics of art and literature, prescriptively as well as descriptively. Hulme's theories are sketchy, his presentation not infrequently confusing, and his poetry mostly fragments. The following pages attempt to analyse his oeuvre, a material hardly anybody has taken the trouble to consider in its entirety, He understood that some form of theory is a useful accompaniment of poetic practice, and, like his Imagist friends, he made the poetic image the focus of his attention. The Imagists were opposed not only to the monopoly of science, *scientia scientium*, which claimed to be able to decide what truth and reality "really" were, but also to the "Tennysonianisms", which, they felt, had made poetry predictable and insipid.

This book attempts to get to grips with the watershed.

I owe Professor Lars Ole Sauerberg my heartfelt gratitude for his advice, encouragement and patience during the process of writing this book.

March 2008

Flemming Olsen

CHAPTER ONE

IMAGISM

NAME. ORIGIN. MEMBERS

Writers and critics of the first and second decades of the 20th century give different versions of the origin of the Imagist movement, and of Hulme's share in it.

The Egoist, an Individualist Review appeared over a period of nearly six years (Jan. 1914 – Dec. 1919). It contained articles about literature, politics, art, and philosophy. It was a very up-to-date periodical, reviewing recently published French literature and eg. assessing the music of Schoenberg. It was a balanced, but at times polemical, avant-garde publication, which devoted the issue of 1st May 1915 to the theory and practice of Imagism[1].

F.S.Flint outlines the history of the Imagist movement: in 1908, Hulme suggested to a friend that they should form a poets' club. The idea materialized, and at the meetings young poets would read their own works. Hulme read his poem about autumn ("A touch of cold in the autumn night")[2]. When Hulme left the club, says Flint, he suggested that the members should meet regularly at a Soho restaurant, the first meeting taking place on 25 March 1909. Hume was the "ringleader", who insisted on "absolutely accurate presentation and no verbiage"[3]. Flint goes on to say that it was in Pound's *Canzoni and Ripostes* (1912) that Hulme's collected poems were published, 35 lines altogether[4]. Hulme had not given his permission.

However, in the prefatory note, Pound gives the reader to understand that he did it for old friendship's sake and rather out of sentimentality. "They are reprinted here" (Pound intimates that Hulme had had them published already) "for good fellowship and for the smallness of their bulk, and for good memory, seeing that they recall certain evenings and meetings of two years gone, dull enough at the time, but rather pleasant to look back upon"[5].

Aldington says in *Life for Life's Sake* that the Imagist movement was born in a teashop in Kensington, and that the term Imagist was coined by Hulme, but that Pound appropriated it[6]. Pound's own version is slightly different: Imagiste (he consistently spells the movement and its practitioners with a final –e) was a word he invented in the tearoom of British museum in October 1912 in order to characterize the quality of H.D.'s poems. "H.D., Imagiste", he wrote at the bottom of a page[7].

However that may be, some credit would seem to be due to Hulme, who perhaps left "his" poetry club in 1909 because Pound had joined it and soon became a prominent member. In 1911, Pound wrote a series of articles for the periodical *New Age* "in illustration of the new method of scholarship"[8], and in 1913 he published "the principles of Imagism" in *Poetry: A Magazine of Verse*, which had been started by Harriet Monroe in 1912. Relations between Hulme and Pound were strained and gradually became characterized by what Flint – who was certain that Pound had borrowed his theories from Hulme – called "polite hostility". Pound preserved "a continuing obligation" to Hulme: as late as in 1938, in *The Townsman*, he is at pains to emphasize that he does not want to diminish the honour due to Hulme, only he did not have a monopoly of literary life in London[9]. And Pound asserted that his own theories ultimately derived from Aristotle.

The members of the Imagist circle pay lip-service to Hulme's pervasive aesthetic preoccupation but they find him at the same time elusive and dogmatic (Wyndham Lewis calls him "a journalist with a flair for philosophy and art, but not a philosopher")[10]. Several of them did not like him as a person. In the eyes of his contemporaries he was a light that soon faded, not only on account of his untimely death. He soon dropped out – or perhaps was dropped out - of the Imagist circle, and he did not contribute to either *Des Imagistes*, which was edited by Pound, or to *Some Imagist Poets*, which was edited by Amy Lowell.

According to Aldington, the Imagists were a group of friends with kindred interests rather than dogmatic principles.. H.D. was by far the most important poet of the group; she was the only genuine Imagist[11]. Her poems, which are often about love, are unrhymed and "bare", ie without linguistic flourishes. Amy Lowell, who wrote some poems for *The Egoist*, is mainly known as an acute and clear-sighted critic of contemporary and foreign poetry (*A Dome of Many-Coloured Glass* (1912), *Six French Poets* (1915), *Tendencies in Modern American Poetry* (1917). The last-mentioned book is an analysis of Imagist principles. Like the others, Aldington was interested in French poetry and worked as the editor of the influential periodical *The Egoist* in the years 1913-1917. Flint translated French poetry (*The Younger French Poets* (1920)), and in his own poetry he experimented with different forms of rhyme. Fletcher was interested in music and painting and wrote poems that are very similar to Hulme's. He was an eager student of French and strove to develop "an attitude towards technique". Gaudier-Brzeska, who died in 1915, aged 24, was originally a painter, but early he began carving in stone: his aim was to "define masses by planes", and his sculptures are characterized by the rugged hardness that was one of Hulme's poetic ideals. Harold Monro criticized the Imagists in *The Egoist:* they are not innovators – most of their poems read like poor translations from French.

A New Note

Industrialism and Positivist science had made only sporadic new ventures into the arts possible. The Victorian literary tradition was felt by most critics to have outlived itself, and Edwardian poetry was notorious for its indsipidity. In *Life for Life's Sake*, Aldington was merciless in his strictures on Georgian poetry: the poets are regional in their outlook and enamoured with littleness; they go on a short trip into the country, where they write a nice little poem about a nice little subject[12].

So there were, around the turn of the century, hopes and expectations that a new note would be struck[13]. The periodical *New Age*, the title of which is symptomatic, was started in 1907 by Alfred Orage. It was a straw in the wind. In 1911, Roger Fry arranged a post-Impressionistic exhibition of paintings in the Grafton Galleries. The pictures defied exact copying of "reality" and were thus an implicit criticism of the artistic ideals that had predominated since the Renaissance. Harold Monro wrote, in the first issue of *The Poetry Review* (1912), that the artist's purpose must be to re-educate a public that had gradually come to misunderstand the uses of poetry[14].

There had been a handful of significant forerunners in the 1890s: Symons' *Silhouettes* (1892) is a series of short impressions of moments that distinguish themselves from the routines of everyday life – fleeting, coloured miniature paintings. The themes and titles are some that occur in Hulme's poems (*After Sunset* and *In Autumn*), and the localities anticipate those we know from the poems of Hulme and the Imagists: London, the Thames, Haymarket. They are nocturnal scenes enveloped in silence and mystery[15]. Symons also wrote some prose criticism that is important though he did not propound any theories in the conventional sense of the word. He was obviously impressed by French literature and criticism (witness his book on the Symbolist movement). He stresses the importance of the "prevailing quality" of a work rather than the details[16], thus echoing Taine. By the same token, in 1894 Beardsley and others started a quarterly that they called *The Yellow Book*. The magazine printed the works of contemporary authors and also featured Beardsley's drawings.

As early as in the 1890s, a few poets had shown an interest in what Farmer calls "l'évocation rapide d'un moment dramatique, pittoresque et isolé"[17]. In connection with a modern translation of the Old English poem *The Seafarer*,

Pound refers to "the New Method in Scholarship", which is "the Method of Luminous Detail", and which is capable of giving "a sudden insight into circumjacent conditions, into their causes, their effects, into sequence and law"[18]. And Whistler's paintings show momentary light effects on the banks of the Thames[19].

THE WORLD AND THE POET

The Imagists acknowledged the premise that reality *is*, but they were convinced that there was a more adequate way of depicting it than that of science. They did not criticize Positivism openly, but they showed what they thought was a necessary and obvious alternative by describing "things as they were" through a series of surprising analogies whose immediate impact would strike the reader, causing him to see and understand the world differently from the scientists' way.

What the Imagists were opposed to was the generalizing and deterministic approach of the Positivists. However, they were neither speculative nor transcendental. Indeed, it can be argued that they fought the Positivists on their own ground by using the technique of observation. They did not suffer from science envy, but they refused to accept causal explanations, and they did not believe that it was possible to arrive at "truth" by the accumulation of scientfic facts. They insisted that the truth they were striving to find had the same value as that of the scientists. They objected to the cult of mechanical regularity, arguing that it was possible to view phenomena individually without being obliged to incorporate them into a necessary and unchangeable relation to other phenomena. It was their contention that it was possible to penetrate more deeply into "reality" by showing, in the form of an arresting image, hitherto unnoticed identities and relations, and our perception of them.

As Abrams points out[20], Aristotle did not find it degrading for poetry to imitate models in the material world. Indeed, he ascribes the origin of poetry to our inborn need of imitating, and of finding pleasure in imitation. The Imagists' poems – including Hulme's - are in the mimetic tradition in so far as they endeavour to render items of what is conventionally understood as reality. Thus, in Hulme's poems we meet eg streets, ships' masts, soldiers and sunsets – but also blood and death. The point is that the poet's acute sense of observation and talent of precise formulation enables him to *discover* (in the etymological sense of the word, viz. "to find something that was hidden, or that people did not know about before" (ALD)) novel aspects of, and relations between, phenomena.

The poet finds himself in our world. He is the unobtrusive recorder, and he does not escape into a transcendental fantasy or a paradisiacal dream. So far from serving merely decorative purposes his images, or image (very often one suffices) are the *raison d'être* of the poem. Unlike the complete picture that science claimed to provide – and scientists never doubted that there was *one* reality – the "alternative reality" called forth by the Imagist poets can only be apprehended in brief glimpses. Reality appears fragmentary and incoherent. The Imagists' use of images is revelatory, their procedure assures the independence, indeed idiosyncrasy, of the scene depicted, and, by that very fact, excludes any possibility of poetic diction. What the Imagists found and wanted to convey was analogous to Bohr's statement to the effect that the result of an experiment is determined by the way the experiment is arranged as well as by the observer's background in the widest sense of the term. The world (like beauty) is in the eyes of the beholder.

The Imagists' world is an avowedly subjective one. Reality is what appears to me. That point is considerably harder to argue than the seemingly objective one of the scientists. Accordingly, their images are comparable to postulates – they would probably retort that so are many of the "laws" of science. It is perhaps no coincidence that no Imagist ever uses the term "reality". Even if they were fond of abstractions, they were not interested in a total view. They did not believe in the "wholeness" offered by science, and they did not go in search of "Ultimate Reality".

Language

The Imagists criticized their Positivist predecessors for having deserted language: by using it for merely denotative purposes they had made language transparent and deluded its users into believing that there is an unalterable one-to-one correspondence between a word and its referent. The Imagists "liberated" language by expanding and sometimes breaking down such "natural" relationships. To Hulme, stars are not only celestial bodies, they are wistful personifications whose faces are pale because they envy the moon its ruddiness. In Saussurean terminology it can be said that the Imagists demonstrated the arbitrariness of the sign, and that they were at least as interested in the *signifiant* as in the *signifié*, which latter had been foregrounded by the Positivists.

Longinus said that the sublime resides in "the stunning image" or in short passages characterized by speed, power, and intensity[21]. The Imagists' technique promoted, and was at the same time conditioned by, the short form and the intense content. Their poems describe momentary situations, and their images capture the reader's attention, forcing him to stop and reflect.

For the moment to gain full impact, precision of formulation was mandatory. The great linguistic discovery that the post-Positivists made was that the link between a word and its referent was not as straightforward as had been assumed by adherents of the scientific method. The denotative element of a word was incapable of taking us beyond what the scientists had looked upon as reality. Nietzsche had warned against the delusion of believing that figures of speech reflect an outside world, ie that they are equivalent to anything in the extralinguistic reality. And Gautier had talked about "extending the boundaries of language…taking colours from all palettes…forcing literary expression of that which is most ineffable"[22].

"The exact word," we read in the preface of the *Imagist Anthology* from 1916, is "that which brings the effect of that object before the reader as it presented itself to the poet's mind at the time of writing the poem". The exact word, then, is based on a subjective response to an objective stimulus. Consequently, the Imagists were keenly aware of what Wittgenstein was later to call "the vagueness of ordinary propositions". Interestingly, Wittgenstein had to resort to the use of images in order to put his message across, and, as was the case with the Imagists, his linguistic creativity was not meant to serve decorative purposes. Later in the 20th century, Austin maintained that language is incapable of giving us absolute certainty. Even in seemingly transparent communication situations, there is a risk of misinterpretation.

The Imagists felt with Pound that "poetic language is the language of exploration", and they agreed with him that using images as nothing but ornamentation is equivalent to bad writing[23]. "There was a lot of talk and practice among us…of what we called the image," said Flint[24]. In the issue of 15 July 1914 of *The Egoist,* Aldington pays tribute to Wyndham Lewis' *Enemy of the Stars* for "the sudden clear *images* which break across it – flashes of lightning suddenly displaying forms above the dark abysmal conflict"[25].

It had not escaped the notice of the Imagists that even Positivist scientists had used figurative language to make themselves understood. The Imagists did not content themselves with recording what they saw, but put "some other seen thing into relation"[26]. Kenner points out that the swift perception of relations was, for Aristotle, the hallmark of poetic genius[27].

FORM

The Impressionist painters had been intensely preoccupied by the technical aspects of their art. In the same way, form played a major part in the theoretical reflections of the Imagist poets. Most of them tended to agree with Flaubert's statement "la forme naît de l'idée"[28]. What mattered was to "trample down every convention that impedes or obscures…the precise rendering of the impulse," said Harold Monro[29]. Regular metre came to be felt more and more as a Procrustes' bed. Rhythm in poetry must correspond precisely with the emotion or shade of emotion to be expressed. A man's rhythm must be interpretative and, consequently, "uncounterfeitable", as Harold Monro put it. And he added that a vast number of subjects cannot be precisely, and therefore not properly, rendered in symmetrical form[30]. That was a standard defence of *vers libre*.

CONTENT

Many of the Imagist poems are about the relationship between poetry and music; they strove with Verlaine, to obtain "de la musique avant toute chose". One implication is that poetry obtains its maximum effect by being read aloud, and that may account for the emergence of many clubs and societies, where poets would read their poems aloud, mostly to critics, other poets, and artists. And they carried the Baudelairean concept of *correspondances* into other arts than music: colours and changing hues (eg of sun and moon) and sounds (eg the splashing of water) are used as ingredients of, or accompaniments to, their images.

They are fond of opposing manifestations of contemporary culture and man, not with a moralizing or nostalgic intent, but just as a fascinating juxtaposition of facts. They are not particularly enthusiastic about nature, especially in its wilder aspects, and they are neither nature mystics nor pantheists. Generally, their choice of subject is nothing out of the ordinary, which makes the total effect of their poems even more striking.

THE IMAGIST PRINCIPLES

Like the Neo-Classicists before them, the Imagists were fond of theorizing about their own background, purpose, and technique. They developed and discussed their assumptions in contemporary periodicals, eg the March 1913 issue of *Poetry*, and in the prefaces of the Imagist anthologies from 1915 and 1916. The Imagists are 1) to use the language of common speech; 2) to use new rhythms; 3) to have total freedom in the choice of subject; 4) to present an image, 5) to write hard and clear poetry; 6) to aim at concentration of purpose.

In *Tendencies*…Amy Lowell explicated and elaborated on some of those themes: using the language of common speech means avoiding the clichés of the old poetic jargon; also inversion should be shunned[31]. Concentration of presentation implies the use of "the exact word which conveys the writer's impression to the reader"[32]. One of her points is that "Imagists fear the blurred effects of a too constant change of picture in the same poem"[33]. She is confident that "the idea clothes itself naturally in an appropriate novelty of rhythm"[34], an alternative version of the Neo-Classical idea of language as the dress of the thought. And in another of her books, *Six French Poets*, she says that the distinguishing feature of the Imagists is that they gave us "picture-making without any comment, eg a contemplation of nature unencumbered by the pathetic fallacy"[35].

Wilkinson is proud that "our generation" does not explain the images: they present them adequately and let them work their spell[36]. To Pound[37], the image is not an idea, "it is a radiant node or cluster…a vortex from which, and through which, and into which, ideas are constantly rushing". "Imagism is presentation, not representation," said Amy Lowell in an article in *Some Imagist Poets*[38]. "An image is real because we know it directly. It is our affair to render the *image* as we have perceived or conceived it"[39].

Contemporary commentators agree on the non-mimetic character of the image, on its intellectual (ie non-emotional) character, and on the instantaneousness of the revelation.. Pound quotes an adequate definition without giving the source: Imagism has been defined as "that which presents an intellectual complex in an instant of time"[40].

Two things strike a modern reader: first the "ordinariness" of the Imagists' subjects: two rather plain young girls walking down a street, and suddenly, as Pound put it, he found "the expression. I do not mean that I found words, but there came an equation… (*his dots!*), not in speech, but in little splotches of colour"[41].

Secondly, we find in Imagist poems a new disparity in the levels of the two ingredients of the image. When a Romantic poet saw eg a sunset, he would use it as a launching pad for serious image-making: it might symbolize death, or it might be used to illustrate the perennial cycle of life, or be invested with some mythological overtones. Hulme associates a sunset with people trotting home from work – and he does not intend to be frivolous or ironic. The "big" sunset is, in more senses than one, pulled down to earth. Appositely, Harold Monro says that the purpose of the Poetry Bookshop that he opened in Devonshire Street in January 1911 was to show people that poetry was written by men alive to their own time[42].

Imagist Criticism of Imagism

The Imagist poets were frequently their own critics. A modern reader will find their evaluations surprisingly frank and precise, and later critics have had little to add. Fletcher wrote in an article in the *Imagist Anthology* from 1916 that one of the cardinal beliefs of the movement was "to present the subject as an image" so that the reader can re-enact for himself "the emotional complex the poet is trying to convey"[43]. As he sees it, "Imagism is an attitude toward technique pure and simple"[44]. Pound called Imagism "chiefly a stylistic movement...a movement of criticism rather than of creation... a type of poetry where painting or sculpture seems as if it were just coming over into speech"[45]. Pound would often refer to the Chinese ideogram, which is a sign and a letter, but which can convey spiritual suggestions. The written characters had, in his opinion, preserved their pictographic element so that the reader would actually see the picture in the ideogram. Hence he concluded that the unit of poetry is an ideogram, the record of a significant glimpse[46]. The emphasis on the picture and the reader's comprehension of it was coming very much to the fore, witness the fascination with the Japanese Noh poems (cf. p. 78), which had unity of image, and whose "emotional pattern was concentrated in the associations evoked by a central concrete figure"[47].

With her usual clear-sightedness, Amy Lowell states that "'Imagism', 'Imagist' refers more to the manner of presentation than to the thing presented...it is a kind of technique rather than a choice of subject"[48]. This is her way of pointing to the non-mimetic aspect of the movement. The originality of their poetry consisted in the choice of a suitable image. They went directly to the point, and the thrill they intended to prompt in the reader was intellectual rather than sentimental. They eliminated the poet's personality and, with that, the kind of private emotion and moralizing that occurs in poet-centred verse. As Hough points out, they broke with an ancient poetic recipe according to which a natural object is presented, followed by some reflections on human experience that arise from it[49].

It was in the periodical *The Egoist* (1914-1919) that the most interesting discussions of the movement took place. Originally the name of the magazine had been *The New Freewoman*, and the editors were two ladies. However, in 1914, the name was changed to *The Egoist* in order to eliminate "the emphasis upon militant feminism"[50]. Aldington was the editor in the years 1913-1917, after which Eliot took over. It was an intellectual periodical, printing reviews and criticism of contemporary music, sculpture, and French literature. Being a balanced, but by no means toothless, publication, it had extensive correspondence columns. It was a tremendous asset for the arts and artists of the second decade of the 20th century to have a magazine that was committed to a debate on what was happening on their very doorstep.

The issue of 1st May 1915 was a specialist Imagist number[51]. As a matter of curiosity it may be mentioned that *The Egoist* did not print anything by, or about, Hulme; nor did it write an obituary when he was killed in the war in 1917.

A few of the contributions may be summarized: on 1st January 1914, Wyndham Lewis wrote an article, *The Cubist Room*, which was inspired by Cézanne. The gist of the article is the author's dissociation from the representational element in the arts. In the issue of 1st May, 1914, Harold Monro gives a terse evaluation of the Imagist movement: it makes use of a restricted vocabulary and a limited number of forms; its practitioners devote a lot of energy to the cult of new forms, their choice of subject is in no way sensational, the city is an obsession for them. However, their way of presentation is new. Their poems are hasty impressions rather than faithful recordings, "the passing effect and its effect on their minds"[52]. They start with "cadences" - a new cadence generates a new idea, but, as Monro sees it, the process should be the other way round. And May Sinclair writes on 1st June, 1915, that the image is the object itself, never a symbol of reality[53].

Undoubtedly Stead is right when he says that the Imagists did not produce a large amount of valuable poetry[54]. The movement simply lost its momentum and died rather suddenly in 1917, the year when the USA joined the First World War. Perhaps the focus of the Zeitgeist shifted. At any rate, 1917 was the year when the last (fourth) Imagist anthology was published.

The Imagists' tenets boiled down to three assumptions: the world exists, is describable, and is well worth describing; the attempts of science to describe reality are insufficient and often misleading; reality is pre-eminently graspable in terms of images and analogies.

Amy Lowell called Imagist poetry "a narrow art, it has no scope, it neither digs deeply nor spreads widely"[55]. Few modern critics would disagree with her on that point. By the same token, she is obviously right when, in an evaluation of H.D.'s poetry, she says that "there are more things in Heaven and Earth than such poetry takes cognisance of"[56]. Equally, the prefaces of the Imagist anthologies are often surprisingly tame. But Glenn Hughes takes an entirely different view: "Imagism is, I believe, destined to command serious consideration from all literary historians of the future"[57]. That prophecy, which dates from a decade after the demise of the movement, has been fulfilled only to a very limited extent: Eliot acknowledged his indebtedness to the Imagists' exploration of the poetic image, and the Deconstructionists' conception of reality shows some points of similarity with that of the Imagists - though they cannot be said to be thankful overmuch!

The Imagists endeavoured to redefine poetry so as to make it worth serious study, and they were the most important group of poets in the years around the First World War. Hynes is unduly harsh in his conclusion: the movement had a name and a manifesto, which made it a contemporary focus of attention, but since its time it has been taken more seriously than it deserves[58].

Imagism represents an intermediate stage between, roughly speaking, Tennyson and Eliot. The difference between the poetry of those two poets would be very hard to account for without the connecting link formed by Imagism. It should not be forgotten that, in 1937, Eliot called Imagist criticism "very important"[59].

Vorticism

The Vorticists are also symptomatic of the mental climate around 1910. In their manifesto, *Blast*, they said that the form of a poem should be "suitable to the emotion the artist wants to express". They combined a cult of the violent image with the dynamism of formal experiments. *Blast* is aggressive and intransigent in its tone, the avowed intention obviously being to "épater le bourgeois". They were pleased to know that they succeeded.

They were interested in all the arts, and they were relevant to the Imagists because they held that "the primay pigment of poetry is the IMAGE" (their capitals)[60], and to Hulme because they were attracted by geometrical shapes, planes, and cubes. As they saw it, only abstraction can give intellectual strength back to art, and they were satisfied that "the inner spiritual force of art uses contemporary forms only as a step by which to progress"[61]. The goal of that forward drive was never specified, and they do not seem to have solved the conflict between an abstract artistic ideal and the concrete images they required in poetry. Pound fell for their all-round intensity, but their concentrated energy soon spent itself, and the quiet exit of the movement after little more than a year is just as symptomatic as its thundery entry.

The following chapters will analyse the Positivist and anti-Positivist theories that were to some extent adopted by the Imagists and Hulme, but which to an even greater extent prompted a violent opposition on their part.

Chapter Two

The Late 19th Century Scientific Model

Introduction

In his *Philosophiae Naturalis Principia Mathematica* from 1687, Newton wrote in the *Præfatio ad Lectorem:* "Utinam ceteræ naturæ phenomena ex principiis mechanicis eodem argumentandi genere derivare licet" (I wish that it will be admissible to derive other natural phenomena from mechanical principles by means of the same kind of argumentation).

That attitude was to be the dominant one within, and also, partly, beyond science for the next two centuries. It came to be *the* underlying motto of the late 19th century set of theories subsumed under the name of Positivism. Owing to the huge authority surrounding Newton's name and the astonishing discoveries made by the use of the Newtonian approach, his procedure was adopted as the only legitimate one. Scientists and philosophers found in it more than a method – it was a tool enabling mankind to move closer towards an understanding of central concepts like "truth" and "reality". The remarkable thing is that even if Newton had only talked of *naturæ* phenomena to be derived from "mechanical principles", the method was used, in the latter half of the 19th century, by non-scientists, eg philosophers and social and literary critics, as well. Therefore, it is appropriate that Silvanus P. Thompson should use the Newtonian quotation as the motto of his huge two-volume biography of William Thomson, who became later Lord Kelvin.

Lord Kelvin

Lord Kelvin, who was born in 1824, is considered the leading figure of English science in the Victorian age. He became a professor at the age of 22, and was raised to the peerage in 1892. Throughout his life he was devoted to scientific experimentation and analysis, and his method closely resembled that of Newton[1].

A statement from his *Introductory Lecture to the Course of Natural Philosophy* (1847) is a good summary of his stance: he strongly recommends "the study of natural philosophy (i.e. the establishment of general laws) in any province of the material world" because of "the importance of its results in improving the physical condition of mankind"[2]. The gentle gliding from "natural philosophy" to "any province of the material world" is significant.

In that passage are contained some of the central ideas of Positivism: observation, generalization, and the deduction of laws. What made the procedure and the ideas so appealing and "evidently right" was "the immense practical importance of the principles of Natural Philosophy at present known", as Kelvin says in the same lecture[3]. As a matter of fact, "at no period in the world's history have the benefits of this kind conferred by science been more remarkable than during the present age"[4]. It was not least the "practical benefits" that made it obvious for the scientific method to be extended beyond science.

The concept of energy played a prominent part in Kelvin's thinking. In an article in *The Cambridge Chronicle* from 1866 he wrote that "the great principles of the conservation of energy teaches us that the material universe moves as a frictionless machine. *Vis viva,* or, as we now call it, Kinetic Energy, is never lost or gained"[5]. In 1884, he gave an address in Montreal intitled *Steps towards a Kinetic Theory of Matter*[6]. So, Bergson's *élan vital* was not his own invention, but a notion that was being discussed even before he began to write, and which, incidentally, became a fulcrum of early 20th century philosophical and poetical thinking. In 1867, Kelvin complimented Helmholz on the latter's "admirable discovery of the law of vortex-motion in a perfect liquid"[7]. The idea of a vortex was used by the early 20th century hyper-dynamic literary movement, the Vorticists. Another instance of scientific terminology appropriating new territory.

Kelvin was a man who eminently summarized "the spirit of the age" within late Victorian scientific thought. He was untiring in his effort to urge his students "to take full advantage of the abstract sciences, mathematics, physics and chemistry – not merely mechanics and the applications of engineering"[8]. He was a modest man, astonished and impressed by the achievements of science – achievements to which he himself greatly contributed. He made ground-breaking discoveries within ocean telegraphy, improvements of the compass, the definition and limitation of geographical time, and the establishment of a thermo-dynamic doctrine. He spent 50 years in an indefatigable quest for a theory of matter. In the 1890s, he was rightly considered the greatest living scientist.

Reality

Kelvin and his contemporaries used the terms "reality" and "nature" almost interchangeably. They held an objective view of reality. Reality is what does not change irrespective of the observer's attitude. The thermic quality of gasses remains unaltered no matter the analyst's angle of approach. The scientists were satisfied that they *found* actually existing conditions of the the surrounding world. Kant had looked upon the concepts of science as tools used by our consciousness to make a comprehensive synthesis of our sense impressions. His point was that the scientists *invented* a picture of the world by virtue of their frames of reference, but that idea did not occur to the scientists of the late 19th century.

Physics and mathematics enabled them to describe the world, and nobody doubted that those two branches of science accounted for something that was already there. They ascribed truth value to what was "evidently" the case. Sometimes validation was felt to be irrelevant: who can validate a rainbow? In the case of issues of speculation, truth was arrived at by the use of what Dewey called "warrantable assertions", ie propositions that can be explicated according to accepted modes of interpretation[9]. Those modes were a combination of inductive generalization and deduction. Kelvin and others were convinced that their procedures enabled them to elicit some of the secrets from reality. Thus, a set of "natural laws" was established, and a rational explanation was given of phenomena that had hitherto been obscure or mysterious.

The late 19th century scientists never tired of refining their instruments and sophisticating their methods. They had no doubt that further developments along the lines laid down by science would take mankind closer to "the way things are". Here we see one of the reasons for the cult of development that runs on into the first decades of the 20th century, but it also goes some way to explain the wave of optimism that was one aspect of late 19th century thinking. That spirit is reflected as early as in Stuart Mill's *Utilitarianism* (1861), in which he says that in order to assess the rightness or wrongness of an act it is imperative to consider its utility value and not the extent to which it accords with some pre-established principles of religion or natural right. The ultimate goal was to create the greatest good for the greatest number of people.

As a matter of fact, the model outlined and the terminology employed by mathematicians and physicists established itself also within biology, sociology, philosophy, psychology, and literary criticism. Earlier in the century Stuart Mill had used it in *A System of Logic* (1843). He wanted to establish common knowledge by means of an inductive approach to observations, and he asserted that the methods of science can be applied within the social sciences and psychology. The scientific model became the mould by which late Victorian thinking was shaped because it was felt to give a valid and true picture of reality.

Chapter Three

The Pervasiveness Of The Model

Ernst Mach

The Austrian physicist, physiologist, psychologist, philosopher and historian Ernst Mach (1838-1916), who was Professor of the History of the Inductive Sciences, said that scientific laws were epistemological shortcuts summarizing observational data.

In his book *Die Leitgedanken meiner naturwissenschaftlichen Erkenntnislehre* (The Essence of my Scientific Epistemology), he states that time and space are problems towards the solution of which physicists are moving closer[1]. He uses sense impressions as his starting-point for our ability to count, weigh, and measure and construct categorizations. Sense impressions, which he calls 'elements', are the only immediate source of physics[2]. Matter to him is a definite order of connections of elements, and the task of science is to analyse those connections, which, as he saw it, was tantamount to finding the laws of nature[3].

Our reflections when we remember sense impressions are the first building blocks of scientific thinking. However, mathematics and physics are not enough: biology, too, has to be included. His purpose in the *Leitgedanken* was to give a biological-economic presentation of scientific experiences. All useful experiential processes are special cases of biologically favourable processes[4]. The activity of science, indeed of all mental life, is "a part of organic living, such that even economy of thought, and the elimination of futile physics, found their deepest justification in biological needs"[5]. But he went further than that: he attempted to bridge the ancient gap between the internal and the external world. In a letter to Wilhelm Ostwald from 1902 he writes that his book *Die Analyse der Empfindungen* (The Analysis of Feelings) "attempts to discover accessible ways from *given* perceptions into what is physical on the one side and into psychological regions on the other"[6].

"Mental and physical processes stand in very close relation to each other", he said in *Lecture on Psychophysics* (1863), and in another letter to Wilhelm Ostwald from 1913 he wrote that "the second law of thermodynamics was not only physically valid, but physiologically and psychologically, too"[7]. Sensations and physical qualities, for which latter Mach also uses the designation 'elements' "are actually identical and only differ in the different ways the relations are considered"[8].

In the Draft Foreword to the Russian translation of *Die Analyse der Empfindungen* (1906/07), Mach calls himself "neither philosopher nor psychologist, but only a physicist"[9]. A modern reader would tend to call him a polymath, but no matter what he devoted his intellectual efforts to, Mach remained faithful to his method. He endeavoured to establish laws and to explain a new fact by means of another, already established one. His procedure was 'economic' in the sense that it was practical and adequate to repay his efforts. Superfluity would be eliminated, and anything smacking of metaphysics was anathema to him[10].

Einstein wrote an obituary of him in *Physicalische Zeitschrift* (1916)[11]. That is evidence of his stature.

Herbert Spencer

Herbert Spencer intended his *System of Synthetic Philosophy*, which was published in ten volumes between 1862 and 1893, to be a synthesis of available knowledge. As he saw it, there exist fundamental laws of development that apply to everything, from particles to societies and cultures. Dynamism was a basic concept in his philosophy, and he saw Darwin's theory of evolution as an empirical confirmation of his own evolutionism. Actually it was he who coined the phrase 'the survival of the fittest'.

The first principles described in great detail in the book of that name (*First Principles*, 1862) are held to be scientific ones. All sciences "germinate out of the experiences of daily life", science being simply a higher development of common knowledge. If science is repudiated, all knowledge must be repudiated with it[12]. Science is endowed with moral overtones: all science is a prevision, and all prevision ultimately helps us to a greater or lesser degree to achieve the good and avoid the bad[13]. Indeed, we have a veritable revelation in science, "a continuous disclosure of the established order of the Universe"[14], and "we cannot rationally affirm the positive existence of anything beyond phenomena"[15].

Science justifies the prevailing optimism: "There are external forces having a tendency to bring the matter of which living bodies consist into that stable equilibrium shown by inorganic bodies"[16]. Everything seems to move towards a state of greater perfection and harmony. Negative factors, decline and stagnation, are consistently ignored by Spencer. His book is an optimistic tribute to the way the universe is organised and to the intelligence of man, which is able to unravel the mysteries and give logical and adequate explanations of concrete phenomena. Spencer does move into abstract speculation now and then, but his starting-point is invariably concrete objects or visible or audible facts.

There are numerous references to "this universal tendency towards a balance"[17]. "All terrestrial changes are incidents in the course of cosmic equilibration"[18]. "Each society displays the process of equilibration in the continuous adjustment of its population to its means of existence"[19]. Spencer goes to great lengths to show the usefulness and applicability of causal explanations borrowed from physics and chemistry. "The phenomena subjectively known as changes in consciousness, are objectively known as nervous excitations and discharges, which science now interprets into modes of motion"[20]. What we regard as mental phenomena actually have their basis in mechanical causes: "The modes of consciousness called pressure, motion, light, heat" can be accounted for by changes of temperature, chemical combinations, etc.[21].

Spencer's category of 'the Knowable' might be taken from a Positivist manifesto: it comprises the indestructibility of matter, the continuity of motion, the persistence of force, and the persistence of relations among forces[22]. He is satisfied that those ideas "are not highly general truths; they are universal truths"[23]. "They are truths which unify concrete phenomena belonging to all divisions of Nature, and so must be components of that all-embracing conception of things which Philosophy seeks"[24]. Spencer's working method is the typcally Positivist one: inductive generalizations showing that phenomena on one level can be subsumed under a common denominator on a higher level because the world of phenomena is governed by the same laws.

The *First Principles* covers multifarious aspects of human knowledge: the solar system, geology, biology, flora and fauna, psychology and sociology, and everywhere the thesis and the procedure are identical: evolution is "a change from the indefinite to the definite…from confusion to order"[25]. The development is from small and simple tools to large and complex machines[26], from a less coherent to a more coherent form[27].

Evolution, which takes up a great part of the book, is taken as a given: by looking at primordial stages in different fields of human knowledge, Spencer traces the forward movement – integration as well as differentiation. He never questions that postulate – he applies it to the development of language as well – and he never gives a reason. Everywhere he sees the effect of a "fluid motion in a certain direction at a certain velocity"[28].

In other passages Spencer acknowledges the difficulty, not to say impossibility, of defining the term motion, which boils down to be a label for an unexplained and unproved aspect of 'the way things are'. Also, he is very reticent with regard to the result of the dynamism. "the end of all the transformations we have traced is quiescence"[29]. So, at some point dynamism stops, and the consequent state is believed to be one of peacefulness. Stasis ultimately replaces flux.

Spencer's oeuvre shows him as a very conscientious philosopher and teacher, who, in his stepwise progression, offers definitions, illustrations, and conclusions. He was obviously proud of the results achieved by his scientific method. Nevertheless the 'first principles' are a series of arbitrarily chosen designations which are unproved – and unprovable – postulates.

Auguste Comte

Auguste Comte is considered one of the founding fathers of sociology. In his *Cours de philosophie positive* (6 vols., 1830-1842), he propounds an evolutionary thesis for man's cognition. There are three stages in an ascending scale of perfection: 1) the theological, 2) the metaphysical, and 3) the positive, where everything is explained with reference to physical laws, ie an ascertained correlation with what is given, or 'positive', in Comte's phrasing. Consequently any search behind empirical data is a return to an abandoned stage in the development of mankind, and the designation given by Comte to the uppermost stage, viz. positive, was adopted as the name of the movement that dominated European thinking in the last four decades of the 19th century.

Comte denied the existence of a metaphysical reality behind the world of the senses, and he maintained that physics had, in his day, reached the positive stage, whereas the study of society was still at the metaphysical stage. He was intent on making sociology a science, but he was perfectly aware of the complexities involved. Actually, in his *Système de politique positive* (1851-1854), he introduces the idea of a secular religion that worships science as the highest divinity.

We are fortunate enough to have an evaluation of Comte's opinions and achievements by one of his influential Positivist contemporaries, viz. John Stuart Mill. The book, *Auguste Comte and Positivism*, was published in 1865, a few years after Comte's death in 1857. By and large, Mill gives an honest and precise account of Comte's ideas, which are obviously in tune with his own. Still, he is a bit annoyed at the extraordinary height to which Comte carries the mania for regulation "by which Frenchmen are distinguished among Europeans"[30]. He sees "the essential principle of M. Comte's political scheme" as being " the necessity of a Spiritual Power, distinct and separate from the temporal government"[31]. That emphasis on the spiritual aspect worried Mill a good deal, and it causes him to take Comte to task for that deviation from the genuine Positivst approach.

Also Comte's *Pensées et préceptes*, edited by Georges Deherne in 1924, is rewarding reading even if the collection, which is an anthology of quotations, is defective in several respects. Thus, no sources are given, and we are not informed about the years of the different quotations. Deherne has arranged them in categories (politics, morals, religion, philosophy), but whether that categorization is Deherne's invention or made by Comte himself remains obscure. The collection lives up to its title: it is emphatically a list of maxims, presented axiomatically and without any exemplification.

Comte regards all facts and events as parts of a constant set of relations, "each one being the invariable consequent of some antecedent condition or combination of conditions"[32]. "Every science aims at foreseeing the succession of phenomena after establishing general laws based on observation"[33]. The word 'positif' is provided with a series of plus value definitions: it signifies "at the same time" real, useful, certain, precise, organic, relative, and even sympathetic[34].

One of the cornerstones of Comte's philosophy is the conviction that the human spirit constantly moves towards unity of method and doctrine; that is for man "the regular and permanent state"[35]. Here - and elsewhere – Comte voices the postulate that science's cult of method and regularity is a characteristic of human nature. Therefore it is impossible to reach a renewal of social theories unless moral and political issues are elevated to the level of the physical sciences by applying the Positivist method[36].

The Positivist method is a combination of objective and subjective procedures *('marches')*, the former enabling us to see the parts, the latter the whole[37]. Concrete explanations would be impossible without the assistance of the human will. Any proposition that is not strictly reducible to a simple statement of a fact, whether particuclar or general, is incapable of offering any real or intelligible meaning[38]. Imagination loses its ancient supremacy and is necessarily subordinated to observation[39]. Both induction and deduction are useful tools. Comte tends to favour induction because deduction is liable to lead the mind astray into metaphysical theories[40].

The method proper to the science of sociology must be, in substance, the same as in all other sciences, viz. the interrogation and interpretation of experience by the twofold processes of induction and deduction[41]. So convinced is Comte of the tenability of his 'positive' hypoteses that Mill quotes him as saying that "there never can have been a period in any science when it was not in some degree positive since it always professed to draw conclusions from experience and observation"[42]. He cites Bacon, Descartes and Galilei in support of his theory. The strength of the positive method, in Comte's view, is that is permits the spontaneous determination of ideas in spite of differences of age, education, climate, language, government, or social customs[43], ie it is universally appplicable.

With effortless ease, Comte applies his theories to politics. Science cannnot govern phenomena – it can observe them and link them, and the same thing goes for politics: it must coordinate all the details relating to the march of civilization, reduce them to the smallest possible number of general facts and link them so as to demonstrate the general law underlying the 'marche'[44]. The intellectual leap is symptomatic: by the time Comte wrote, politics had no method of its own, and so, quite naturally, he adopted the one that had yielded astounding results in other areas.

The social sciences (the very name is symptomatic) are subject to the same laws as physics and chemistry: "the human spirit has elevated itself to think in a Positivist way about all physical, chemical, and psychological matters – why should it them reason theologically and metaphysically on social pheno–mena?"[45]. The way for the social sciences to go is obviously to become Positivist.

Even religion "must be something by which to systematize human conduct"[46]. Ethical science will tell everybody where the limits of altruism are[47]. Religion and morals are subject to the same laws as science. Comte does not refer to a possible hereafter, and morals seem to be guided by enlightened self-interest and not based on religion. However, moral science is the principal one among sciences.

Reality exists, and it is independent of our intervention[48]. What exists can only be fully understood if it is connected with what goes before and what comes after[49]. And "what is known about a subject only becomes a science when it is made a connected body of truth; in which the relation between the general principles and the details is definitely made out, and each particular truth can be recognized as a case of the operation of wider laws"[50].

Truth consists in establishing sufficient harmony between our subjective ideas and our objective impressions[51]. The subjective/objective dichotomy is referred to again and again by Comte. "The universal principle of positive logic is to subordinate practically (*convenablement*) the subjective to the objective so that we always construct the most simple hypothesis capable of showing the totality of the observation"[52]. Simplicity is justified on moral grounds and 'demonstration' is indispensable: the impact of demonstration is far beyond what has been hitherto supposed. If demonstration occurs, aberrations will stop[53]. But the subjective element plays a crucial part, for without theoretical abstraction we should never be able to establish the general laws that enable us to foresee where intervention will be beneficent[54].

Even if he has no doubt about the necessity of working along scientific lines,

Comte says that the ordinary citizen need not go into abstruse detail: he should only study the planets that are visible to the naked eye, and "the motions and mutual actions of sun, earth and moon are sufficient"[55]. As Mill puts it: "He would pare down the dimensions of all the sciences as narrowly as possible"[56], and he is worried "lest people should reason, and seek to know, more than enough"[57].

Comte's attitude was not that of a fanatic with a one-track mind who looked down on ordinary people. He was simply concerned with the practical aspect of things: why burden your brain with something that was superfluous? And the scientist had a distinct moral responsibility: "the exercise of the intellect, as of all our other faculties, should have for its sole object the general good"[58]. "The good of others is the only inducement on which we should allow ourselves to act", and "moral discipline consists in cultivating the utmost possible repugnance to all conduct injurious to the general good"[59].

Comte did not doubt that 'the march of civilization' was subject to an unchangeable law based on 'the way things are'[60]. As Mill wrote, Comte did not have the presumption to boast that he possessed the sum total of knowledge – but he did not doubt that he was an infallible judge about what knowledge was worth possessing. And he did not believe that mankind had reached in all directions the extreme limits of useful and laudable inquiry[61].

Hippolyte Taine

Today there is a movement that takes 'les sciences morales' closer to 'les sciences naturelles', giving the former "the principles, precautions and directions of the latter, providing them with the same degree of substantiality, and assuring them the same progress," wrote Taine in his *Philosophie de l'art* (ten lectures given between 1865 and 1869)[62]. He is convinced that his age is witnessing a profound and universal change in the minds and conditions of people, unequalled in any century. The discoveries of the 'positive sciences' are multiplied by the day, and everything has changed for the better: in every respect man cultivcates his intelligence and increases the amenities of his life[63]. The philosophy aspect of the book (cf. the title) consists in speculations on the influences of outward circumstances on the production of works of art.

The interest in, and dependence on, the scientific method was with Taine right from the beginning, and it permeates everything he wrote. As early as in his youthful essay on Livy from 1855 (he was born in 1828), he says that he is looking for "a dominant characteristic quality, from which everything can be deduced geometrically"[64]. In a later work he attacks contemporary French philosophy for being political, moralizing, and verbose. The duty of philosophy, he states, is to ascertain facts, deduce laws, and prove them[65].

Taine is particularly fond of biological analogies: just as plants thrive best in a certain temperature, the creation of a work of art requires "a *moral* temperature, which makes a selection among different kinds of talent, allowing only some of them to develop, and excluding others". Darwin had not lived in vain. The situation in contemporary France is compared with the life of insects: the dangerous point is where the caterpillar changes its form and becomes an insect. But you do not criticize an insect's metamorphosis, and in the same way social changes (Taine is referring to the situation in France from the end of the 18th century to his own day) should be above criticism and moralizing (*Origine de la France contemporaine*)[66].

By the same token, societies are living organisms like trees: they grow in an environment and are subject to diverse influences. Accordingly, everything in a society cannot be totally transformed or scrapped[67]. The living body is a colony of mutually dependent cells; in the same way the acting spirit is a colony of mutually dependent images. Taine talks about "our intellectual machine", and he rejects words like, reason, will, intelligence, and personal force: they are literary metaphors. The living human body consists of cells of various kinds which are capable of development and are influenced by opposition to, or assistance from, neighbouring cells[68]. Each notable individual possesses a dominant quality (*qualité maîtresse*) plus some secondary ones – just as within biology there are dominant and secondary qualities[69].

Taine was an art historian and a literary critic by profession, but also those disciplines are treated by him as if they were scientific objects of analysis: within history and aesthetics the point is to start from an experience and, by working on it, find some abstract features which can be organized. The procedure is, as in natural science, to mutiply and connect generalizations[70]. Different people's tastes go beyond individuals and establish a serious and solid basis for scientific examination[71]. Taine was so immersed in scientific thinking that, quite naturally, he applied the patterns of science to an area that has conventionally been considered significantly different from science, viz. literature. Characteristically, the starting-point of his reflections is a scientific analogy, not history or literature *per se*.

As far as method is concerned. Taine advocates the one that had been triumphant within biology and zoology: to collect and analyse various specimens, distinguish their elements, give a precise account of their relations, and classify them so as to discover their internal hierarchies[72]. In the Introduction to his *Histoire de la littérature anglaise* he outlines the method he intends to adopt: collection of facts should be followed by a search for causes. The point is that facts are to serve a purpose, viz. the establishment of regularities. The parallel is pursued: let's look for simple backgrounds for moral qualities as we look for them in the case of physical qualities[73].

Plants and animals obey laws: eating, reproduction, etc; those laws can be found by methodical observation and experimentation, and everything that exists should be studied like that[74]. Actually his famous tripartite system accounting for literary creation was inspired by his observation of a living oak-tree: understanding of the tree, he realized, is based on 1) its race, ie the latent potentialities contained in its embryo; 2) the environment in which it grows, and 3) the moment in which it finds itself. This categorization, *la race, le milieu, le moment*, is inductively extended to apply to animals and human beings as well – and to art forms and literature, too[75].

Taine was convinced of the forcefulness of the inductive method. He pointed to the impressive results obtained by mathematics and science by using it. In the preface to *De l'intelligence* he paid tribute to John Stuart Mill for having taught him the far-reaching implications of the inductive method: from partial and specific regularities we move on to general and total regularities, and that leads us to the idea of the overall regularity of natural objects. An introductory suggestion leads us to an axiom, which is ultimately verified[76]. As evidence of the superiority of the inductive method Taine cited the results achieved within different areas, also non-scientific ones: man had managed to control nature, reform society, improve his conditions, and adjust things according to his needs[77].

Race is rather vaguely definded: it is the innate and inherited qualities that man carries with him, and which are visible in his temper and the build of his body[78]. The characters of races are above the characters of peoples: certain general features point to ancient affinities between nations of a different genius[79]. This doubtful mixture of biology and psychology is, in other passages, even more watered down so as to designate people speaking the same language.

'Le milieu' can be natural as well as human: in his *Histoire de la littérature anglaise* Taine starts by giving a description of the English landscape before he proceeds to characterize the race. English literature, then, is seen as a natural and expected function of 'milieu' and 'race'.'Institutional milieus' are family, society, governement, education, and religion. 'Le moment' is about time, whereas 'le milieu' is about space: an artist is indebted to his own age as well as to his predecessors. But, paradoxically, 'le moment' is also a movement that changes, be it ever so slightly, the facts of a situation[80].

On top of the three, Taine postulates the existence of a fourth characteristic, viz. 'la faculté maîtresse'. It is a fairly intangible concept of a psychological kind. What it boils down to is the creative artist's talent, his ability to permeate his work with some distinctive features. The Neo-Classical critics of the 17th century called it *je ne sais quoi*. Taine makes frequent references to it, without ever giving an unambiguous definition.

Taine's theory building is beset with problems. It is true that he does establish concepts and make intelligible relations between them[81]. But his terminology is vague, and even though he was a historian and a literary critic he uses a biological paradigm as his basic pattern. His over-confident use of induction and deduction causes him to make hazardous analogies between plants, societies, human beings, and literary works. The differences between an oak-tree and a literary work are greater than the similarities between the two. Besides, his deterministic belief makes him reduce the influence of the human factor. His intelligence told him that *race, milieu* and *moment* do not yield an exhaustive account either of the creation or of the quintessence of a literary work; to put it differently, this was an area where a purely Positivist approach did not lead to 'the truth'. Taine never drew that conclusion, but he supplemented the basic cornerstones with a completely arbitrary superstructure that he called 'the master quality', a non-scientific concept allowing room for a subjective element. That *faculté* was made to serve as a jack-of-all-trades to do the job that the other three were obviously incapable of performing. However, it does not take us any closer to the creative process, nor is it of any assistance in demonstrating *why* one literary work ranges as a masterpiece whereas another does not. As a matter of fact, the term is so vague that it becomes a tautology. On the whole, Taine is weak on terminology: 'historical', 'experimental' and 'positive' tend to become synonymous.

Taine's artistic philosophy is greatly indebted to science: the reader or critic must try to find *le caractère essentiel* in a work of art – a quality from which all the others, or at least most of them, can be deduced according to 'fixed relations'[82]. However, the interesting thing is that he claims that art can do something that nature is sometimes unable to do: in a work of art 'different features' link themselves to each other, and their *convergence* makes a profound impression on man. That convergence is sometimes missing in nature, but never in the works of great artists. Hence eg a character in a novel can become more powerful than a real human being[83].

Chapter Four

Positivism And Its Limitations

Positivism

The term Positivism is loosely applied to the currents within philosophy and the theory of science that take science as the basis and ideal of all human cognition. The word was coined by Saint-Simon and adopted by his pupil Comte, who used it about the way of thinking he borrowed from science, and which became very influential in late 19th century intellectual life. Science was, as Nordmann puts it, regarded as a simplified, abstract and unifying representation of reality. Hence the Positivists were averse to any kind of metaphysical speculation[1].

Nerval wrote in *Le Christ aux Oliviers. Les Chimères* (1854): "God is dead, Heaven is empty. Cry, ye children, for you have no longer any father". More than half a century later, Nietzsche expressed the same thought in *Also sprach Zaratustra* (1911). To a large extent, the Positivists used science as a substitute for God, for it was supposed to do justice to all the data within the range of human knowledge. It is not difficult to understand the feeling of wonder and exhilaration that filled the Positivists when they realized that human reason and the universe were at one, and that reason was a unique product of the human brain since it proved to be able to read 'the book of nature'

Taine said that it was the task of the sciences to evaluate the features that make up human beings [2], and according to Comte, religion must be based on philosophy, which, in its turn, must be beholden to science[3]. "To ask whether science is substantially true is much like asking whether the Sun gives light", wrote Spencer in his *First Principles*[4]. What was in accordance with 'reality', as the Positivists saw it, was held to be true, and since the Positivists had no doubt that science gave a correct picture of truth, there was no truth beyond that of science.

'The positive' means 'the given', ie what is observable, actual, real – with an undertone of what is useful. The Positivists again and again refer to the indispensability of observation and experience. John Stuart Mill proceeded empirically: whenever possible, he based knowledge on observation, and Taine asserted that the different kinds of knowledge derive from perception, which furnishes pictures to the imagination and the memory[5]. Induction and deduction were favourite methods with the Positivists – deduction because it was a frequently used operation within mathematics.

The purpose was, in all cases, to arrive at a generalization. Generalizations were elevated to the status of laws, and they formed the basis of theory-making. Comte was aware of the leap from practice, which is necessarily particular, to theory, which is always general[6]. The 'positive' facts were arranged according to their succession, similarities, and relations; those relations were held to be constant, ie always identical in identical circumstances. As Mill puts it in his book on Comte: "The constant resemblances which link phenomena together, and the constant sequences which unite them as antecedent and consequent, are termed their laws"[7]. Phenomena are explained as manifestations of those laws. Mach said that we collect sums of sense observations in intellectual rules whose value is determined by the degree of precision with which they represent the sense observations.

The Positivist never questioned the reliability of their senses, and it did not occur to them that different people do not necessarily have identical sense impressions of the same object. The results they achieved thanks to their working methods were uniform and showed the Positivists a universe characterized by order and regularity. But also in sublunary matters they attempted to establish – and claimed to find – systems of order. Comte's theory of the three stages of the development undergone by any society is a case in point. Another is Taine's tripartite division of the conditions for the creation of a work of art. Taine also made a hierarchy of works within the individual arts.

With their emphasis on 'the given', it was inevitable that the Positivsts should be anti-metaphysical. "The direct determining cause of every phenomenon is not supernatural, but natural", said Comte[8]. And their adherence to induction and deduction to the exclusion of more intuitive procedures made them staunch determinists. "The physicist has nothing to look for beyond sensory phenomena", wrote Mach. And he went on to ask a rhetorical question that is characteristic of the mental climate of the age: is there a reality independent of our consciousness? Is it necessary to find out – at best that is the province of the philosopher – and what purpose does it serve?[9].

Positivism included a theory of historical development, evolutionism. Darwin's theories acquired an almost religious status, and their emotional appeal and theoretical impact were tremendous. Using their favourite technique of induction, the Positivists effortlessly transferred the findings within biology to other areas of knowledge. It is not only that several philosophers (eg Taine and Comte) used biological analogies, it is also that terms like, energy, dynamism, movement, force, and flux became household words also in the humanities.

They even penetrated into politics, where dynamism and development were important motives underlying imperialism.

What people tended to overlook was that Darwin's evolutionism was a hypothesis, not gospel truth. And, inevitably, the more removed the Darwinian model became from biology proper, the more watered down it became. The remarkable thing is that a no-nonsense 'school' like Positivism should unhesitatingly adopt what, in the humanities, bore a strong resemblance to metaphysical postulates. However that may be, the consequence was that the opinion formers, no matter what area of human knowledge was their speciality, worked according to the same paradigm and used the same terminology. What is more, the idea of development and flux survived the death of Positivism and remained one of the key concepts of a convinced anti-Positivist like Bergson (cf. p. 69 et seq.).

"It is a truth that change is universal and unceasing," said Spencer in *First Principles*[10]. What made the idea of change so palatable was that, as Darwin had shown, the movement went from what was lower towards what was higher. So, development came to be synonymous with progress, improvement. Thus, Comte was convinced that there is a natural evolution in human affairs and that the evolution is an improvement, viz. the progress towards an ascendancy over our animality[11]. For the results of science were not only impressive, they were also useful and evidently man-friendly. The general conditions of mankind had obviously been improved, and man, his needs and his well-being, were increasingly focused on. "All species of animals and plants which are useless to man should be systematically rooted out," demanded Comte[12].

The Positivists saw an unbroken line of increasing success within science and technology and the way society was arranged from the Renaissance and onwards. Spencer was convinced that "there is progress towards equilibrium"[13]. That state was supposed to be one of unqualified bliss, even if no details were given. Stuart Mill saw it as a society's duty to create the greatest good for the greatest possible number. Accordingly, all individuals should be free to do whatever they like so long as it does not inflict harm on others. An understandable wave of optimism permeates Positivist thinking.

Limitations

In that golden age of science, interest in art was bound to be more hesitant and less unequivocal. The Positivists' reservation was caused by their realization that the scientific method did not seem immediately applicable to eg literature and painting. Therefore, there is an atmosphere of the appendix or the footnote about the respect that some of them claim to feel in the presence of artistic masterpieces. For example, it is only in the very last stage of Mach's theory building that poetic imagination and imagery are at all referred to. And when it does come, the treatment is cursory and almost reluctant.

By the same token, in spite of their predilection for systems and generalizations, few of the Positivists attempted to establish anyting like a coherent theory of art. In his *Causeries du Lundi* (1851-62), Sainte-Beuve gave a series of literary portraits. His aim was to bring to light the personality behind the work, but, characteristically, although he proceeded intuitively and scorned the use of theories and doctrines, he considered himself a Positivist and saw his activity as a contribution to scientific psychology. Literary criticism was to him a science-derived pursuit, a kind of humanistic anatomy.

Comte has very little to say about humanistic activities. He speaks with contempt about psychology[14], and he makes it abundantly clear that observation takes precedence over imagination. In one of his *Pensées* he pays lip-service to art, which is "destined to cultivate our instincts of perfection. Hence its range is just as extensive as that of science"[15]. Science is the basis of comparison. However, that seeming parity-of-esteem approach is not followed by any reference to, or description of, a concrete work of art.

The Positivists saw literature in terms of something else, eg social conditions. The attitude is reminiscent of that of modern ideological criticism, which endeavours to analyse the attitude to life formulated in literary works, and to relate them to the surrounding society. As Taine saw it, the creation of literary works was largely determined by historical and geographical factors. His categorizations are specious, but superficial, and he never judges a literary work on its own merits. Everybody acknowledges the superiority of Dante and Shakespeare, he says, and successive centuries cannot go wrong: some truths are undisputed – but he does not go into any detail about the 'undisputed superiority' of Dante or Shakespeare. He recommends something resembling 'close reading', and he says that the point of literary criticism is to look into the works and find out why and by what means they have become outstanding[16]. However, his own achievements are not always convincing – perhaps because, in his opinion, "metaphoric style is inexact style": having recourse to images means that you abandon the obvious support of an exact expression. On the other hand he praises the "summary of ideas contained in a vivid image, or in an apparent paradox, the more so because it is short and, in a flash, thoroughly illuminates a situation or a character"[17].

The attacks that have been launched against Positivism have not always been fair. The Positivists were not dry-as-dust materialists or unimaginative determinists, and most of them suspected that the world picture given by science might not contain the whole truth. It is noticeable that, in their writings, scientists often resorted to metaphoric language to put their message across or to illustrate or explain their theories. The questions they put to Dame Nature were answered – perhaps because they formulated them the way they did. They felt that the method of weighing, counting, and measuring had taken them closer to some important truths about the surroundsing world, and they were aware that what did not come within the purview of science was something different. However, they were honest and clear-sighted enough to admit and acknowledge its existence, indeed, as far as the philosophers were concerned, perhaps even to grant it equal status. To a greater or lesser extent, all the Positivists endeavoured to come to grips with some fundamental problems that were felt to be urgent, but which the scientific method was incapable of solving. To the scientists, who loved definitions and based many of their explanations on causal relationships, the questions that posed themselves were the definition and nature of concepts like motion, force, and development, and the nature and quality of a possible First Cause. The philosophers and literay critics, who were less at ease with purely mechanical explanations, were suspicious of absolute truths and were trying to determine the nature and province of the imagination.

The Scientists

"The Positivist spirit endeavours to determine how, not why," said Comte[18]. However, already Pascal had questioned the adequacy of the method used within mathematics and logic: in those systems, imporatant truths were liable to be overlooked. The Positivist scientists, too, realized that their methods and attitudes left large areas of life unnoticed and undescribed. Some of them went further in that they questioned the capacity of language to characterize and describe the thing conventionally called reality.

Ernst Mach is an interesting case because he was a physicist as well as a philosopher. He was suspicious of metaphysics, and yet he wanted to explore it so as to make it meaningful by finding relations to what is sensory or empirical[19]. On the other hand he was convinced that "our physical concepts take us very close to facts, but cannot be regarded as the final expression of facts"[20]. The adequate representation of facts was a goal, and while striving to reach it, science was moving in the realm of conjectures[21]. The concepts and theories of physics represent an intellectual short-cut – Mach uses the expression *denkøkonomisch*[22]. What we call laws is made up of simplification, schematization, and idealization[23]. The thing-in-itself (*das Ding as sich*) is not only unreachable, it is also illusory[24].

Mach recognizes the existence of the imagination: it is the *differentia specifica* for the human being[25]. The work and the role of the imagination are alone in a position to lead us away from what we habitually expect again and again[26]. He is prepared to acknowledge that "abstractions and the acting of phantasy do the main work in the finding of new knowledge"[27]. He who lets his imagination roam crosses the line of what is *really* possible to the objects that are *logically* impossible[28]. He admits that "only poetic imagination makes it possible to discover new methods and problems". However, in the estimation of the value of such findings, he only goes halfway to slackening the Positivst rein: the success depends on the extent to which those new methods and problems are adjusted to the existing theoretical structure, or, sometimes, break it[29].

Also, the Positivist scientists were hesitant or uneasy where religious and moral issues were concerned. Thus, Lord Kelvin was a religious man who believed in a Creative Power and an overruling Providence[30]. But life and physics are separated in watertight compartments: life is outside the range of physics, and he states, somewhat cryptically, that "life does not proceed from dead matter, but from life"[31]. He recommends the study of Greek, and in an address to an audience of students in 1892 he says that the task of the university is not only to qualify them for a profession, but also "to give a possession for life that rust could not corrode, nor moths eat, nor thieves break through and steal"[32] – without however, going into detail about what such a 'possession' consists of.

THE PHILOSOPHERS

It is characteristic that in their hesitations and doubts about Positivism, the philosophers do not let go of the angles of approach and the terminology of the sciences. When Taine remonstrates with some Positivists over their attitude to art, he speaks in biological terms. Positivist philosophers may estmate and criticize the set of doctrines from within, but none of them offers anything like an alternative vision, either in part or as a whole.

Spencer points to the fact that many of the technical and abstract terms used by scientists are actually nothing but convenient labels, They pretend to explain, but give an arbitrary name to something that remains unknown: "For though the *law* of gravitation is within our mental grasp, it is impossible to realize in thought the *force* of gravitation"[33]. In another passage he says: "These universally co-existent forces of attraction and repulsion must not be taken as realities, but as symbols of the reality"[34].

Comte took exception to unnecessary complications of the explanations – that way madness lies ("*réellement une tendance vers la folie*")[35]. We have to recognize, he says, that "the laws of the real world are too numerous and too intricate in their working to be correctly traced and represented by our reason"[36]. And he considers the pedantic anxiety shown for complete proof by scientific men "their greatest aberration"[37]. However, it was not only that their attempts to render things intelligible landed scientists in pedantry and talk, it was also that many of their efforts were exaggerated or yielded insufficient results. Like metaphysics and religion, science has *des inconvénients* as well as *des avantages,* and, if pursued to unnecessary lengths, results tend to become harmful[38]. If science is raised to the level of being a goal instead of being a tool, it becomes morally dangerous[39]. Spencer sings the same song: "Knowledge of the lowest kind is *un-unified* knowledge. Science is *partially-unified* knowledge; Philosophy is *completely-unified* knowledge"[40].

Spencer blames science for falling short on crucial issues like the nature of the First Cause and of poetic imagination – but he offers no suggestion himself. His reason tells him that "evolution has an impassable limit"[41], but science does not help him to get beyond that limit. Equally, "unceasing deductions finally result in the cessation of motion"[42], and he is completely at a loss with regard to what happens then.

Comte warns thinkers against a too severe scrutiny of scientific laws[43]. He attacks one of the cornerstones of the scientists, viz. objectivity. There is no abolute division between 'observing' and 'reasoning'; no observation can or should be purely objective. To Comte, unimpeachable objectivity came second to subjective usefulness, ie "the affording of faciles to the mind for grouping phenomena"[44]. He says aloud what scientists only whispered, viz. that the making of syntheses is a subjective operation, for which reason the end and purpose of positive science leaves "some degree of liberty…to our intelligence"[45]. And if we insists on "ideality", we must calculate with a "considerable margin of indeterminateness"[46].

As a matter of fact, all the Positivist philosophers are uneasy about the tenet that truth is immediately derivable from speculation on the basis of observation of 'what is'. They had a feeling that there must be 'something' above or behind what observation and the consequent establishment of laws could teach us. According to Charles Peirce, it is impossible for man to attain unmediated access to what is conventionally called reality. Spencer says that "it must be remembered that the connexion between the phenomenal order and the ontological order is for ever inscrutable"[47]. As he sees it, all 'phenomena' are interpretable in terms of "Matter, Motion, and Force", but he is aware that those words are merely symbols: an "Unknown Reality" underlies both "Spirit and Matter", and "even the sphere of the phenomenal cannot be penetrated to its confines"[48]. According to Comte, even "our healthy theories" can offer nothing but "permanently imperfect approximations" to the nature of "*le Spectacle extérieur*". That, however, should not deter us from simplifying and embellishing our hypotheses[49].

Spencer is at pains to stress the relativity of our knowledge: thus we cannot comprehend whether time and space are limited or unlimited[50]: the two are "wholly incomprehensible", and "the same goes for Matter and the transfer of Motion"[51]. We have only "an indefinite consciousness of an absolute reality transcending relations"[52]. Comte agrees: "We have no knowledge of things except Phænomena; and our knowledge of Phænomena is relative, not absolute. We know not the essence, nor the real mode of production, of any fact, but only its relation to other facts in the way of succession or similitude...The laws of Phænomena are all we know respecting them.

Their essential nature, and their ultimate causes, either efficient or final, are unknown and inscrutable to us"[53].

The Positivists approached the problem of the origin of the universe cautiously. As Spencer puts it: We find "insurmountable difficulties rise up before us on all sides...We find ourselves obliged to make certain assumptions; and yet we find these assumptions cannot be represented in thought"[54]. The Positivist philosophers agree on one point: the distinguishing features of the universe are order and harmony. That order, says Comte, is essentially beyond our understanding, and all we can do is to attempt to modify it to our advantage. The awareness of such an order serves as a brake on our spontaneous tendency to form our opinions according to our hopes and fears[55]. And Spencer sees in every organism a tendency "to return to a balanced state"[56].

The Positivist philosophers were obviously in a dilemma regarding the nature and characteristics of reality: on the one hand, the multifarious instances of order that they saw around them led them to infer the existence of an even higher and more perfect order, of which the things that surround us are manifestations. On the other hand, they become mealy-mouthed and often self-contradictory when they attempt to describe that higher order. If it was a state of permanent equilibrium, it was contrary to one of their favourite ideas that they claimed to see illustrated wherever they turned, viz. dynamism – the opposite of permanence. Therefore Spencer says later in the book: "That its (sc. the Universe's) state must change is clear: the irregular distribution of it being such as to render even a temporary moving equilibrium impossible"[57] In his preface to *Les philosophes classiques du xix siècle* Taine admits that the Positivists know nothing about "the cause of life". And he proceeds to quote Hegel with approval: "Beyond all inferior analyses which are called science, there might be a superior analysis called metaphysic which would gather laws and types under a universal formula"[58].

The Positivist philosophers felt that they were treading on treacherous ground when their scientific curiosity pushed them to tackle the question of a possible Beyond. They were honest enough to admit that they would have to resort to conjectures if they wanted to pursue the investigation. Accordingly they resigned and agreed with Spencer that "the Power which the Universe manifests to us is inscrutable"[59] and took comfort in the thought that "the knowledge within our reach is the only knowledge that can be of service to us"[60].

The concept of an Absolute was difficult to fit into the Positivist assumptions. Thus Taine was prepared to recognize the existence of two kinds of truth: besides intellectual truth there is another, determined by the reader's or spectator's emotions[61]. Once more the purely scientific approach gets the worst of it. By the same token, Comte states that there is no "*régime politique*" that is absolutely preferable to all others: the institutions that are good in one age may be bad in another[62]. However, as Spencer shrewdly observes, "to say that we cannot know the Absolute is, by implication to affirm that there *is* an Absolute"[63]. Unfortunately the human intelligence is incapable of acquiring absolute knowledge - we must be satisfied with "Phænomena"[64].

The Positivist philosophers used various designations for the mysterious 'something' of which they recognized the existence: the Absolute, the Unknowable, the Incomprehensible, Ultimate Reality, for example – but none of them uses the word God. Spencer and Comte are the only two philosophers in whose oeuvre we find any reference at all to religion. They pay lip-service to it in a few brief passages, and they hesitatingly admit its possible value, but they do not give the slightest hint that the origin and workings of the universe may be of a divine nature. Ultimate reality was to them so lofty a concept that is could only be imagined as having the qualities of a scientifically arranged universe – raised to a higher power, of course, than evidenced by its manifestations here on earth. Reality was alluring, tempting investigation, but it was entirely devoid of moral overtones.

"Are phænomena due to the variously-conditioned workings of a single force, or are they due to the conflict of two forces?" asked Spencer[65]. The thought as well as the terminology are characteristic: a force is a dynamic entity, not an elevated divinity who rests content after His work of creation, and the idea of two conflicting forces is Darwinian in inspiration. The thought is pursued elsewhere in Spencer's *First Principles:* "Religion expresses some eternal fact; while science is an organized body of truths, ever growing, and ever purified from errors"[66]. Hence religion is obviously not the final answer. Ultimate ideas within religion are no better than ultimate ideas within science: both of them are "merely symbols of the actual, not cognitions of it"[67].

Comte ventures a step further, yet without committing himself whole-heartedly: "And yet, even if the natural order is in all respects very imperfect, the creation of it is better reconciled with the assumption of an intelligent will than of a blind mechanism"[68]. However, in a later passage he checks himself, for of course religion should know its place: "The different religions suffer from theoretical stupidity, but they preserve, in different degrees, a moral effectiveness which the Positivst religion honours and develops – for even the most imperfect ones range above divine scepticism"[69].

Man's place in the universe was not discussed. It was never suggested that he was created in God's image, yet he was indisputably the one who was meant to, and capable of, solving the riddles of "the things that are". The human reason takes pride of place with both scientists and philosophers, confidently and unswervingly. Nobody contested its position – had it not furnished convincing evidence of the way the universe worked, and had it not improved people's material conditions perceptibly? Emotions could not be completely ignored, of course, but they held a definitely inferior position and were looked askance at by many who feared that they might become uncontrollable.

Science formulated more and more laws, a fact which was equated with progress. However, crucial questions with regard to the status of the laws lay outside the scope of Positivist thinking: were the laws simply 'there', waiting for somebody to formulate them, and, if so, who or what had arranged things in such a way that man could deduce facts about the universe? The laws were seemingly clear and non-contradictory. It was as if they had actually been planned for man's benefit. Few of the Positivists ventured to draw any inferences regarding the existence or the intervention of an 'intelligent will'.

Another equally important question, viz. the meaning of life, was only tackled indirectly by the Positivists. Most of them agreed with Stuart Mill and saw happiness in purely materialistic terms: the more material progress, the greater happiness. Morality was established, not on the basis of religion, but on the premises of Positivism. That is not to say that the Positivists were thoroughly selfish and cynical: Stuart Mill took up the cudgels for women and advocated education, and Taine discussed the problem of art – actually the only Positivist thinker to do so at any length.

In a series of articles that he contributed to periodicals in the 1850s and 1860s – born in 1828, he was still a young man then – Taine maintains the independence of art vis-à-vis science: science aims at truth, art at beauty[70], but he does not attempt to identify the two, as Keats did in *Ode on a Grecian Urn*. Characteristically, Taine does not attack the scientific approach; only, it has a terminology that is different from that of art. Whenever he talks abour art, Tains uses words with a large extension and a small intension. The information value is very limited, as when he says that if a person is to be able to enjoy "*la grande peinture*", he must possess a certain amount of culture[71]. The creation of a work of art demands "a general situation" a coincidence of circumstances to which the artist feels subjected. That situation creates needs, talents, and feelings in the artist[72].

Taine bases his evaluation of individual works of art on postulates that he never attempts to substantiate. His idiosyncratic concept, "the predominance of a master talent", is an escape from a purely deterministic systematization, but it is also a big vessel into which a good many ingredients can be poured; poetic imagination, about which he has very little to say, seems to be one of them. For all his knowledge of the history of art and his familiarity with individual works, Taine has little to say about the understanding and appreciation of art. As a good Positivist, he is an expert on empirical facts, but he does not get very far beyond them. In fairness it should be added, though, that none of the leading Positivists dug any deeper.

Most of the Positivist scientists and philosophers were uneasy about the insufficiency of their methods and 'laws' as far as non-scientific areas were concerned. But they did not place themselves outside the paradigms and criticize their own procedures, let alone establish a genuine alternative. They sophisticated their approaches, but they did not deviate from the beaten track. There were questions that could not be answered, a fact which they were honest enough to admit, and to which virtually all the influential Positivists resigned themselves.

Chapter Five

Countercurrents

Though the latter half of the 19th century was dominated by the Positivst spirit, it did not hold uncontested sway. The discussions surrounding the conception of the world and reality had been based on a consensus with regard to what questions could be asked, and what could be acknowledged as truth. But towards the end of the century that consensus began to be shaken. As was mentioned in the previous chapter, there were issues within the realm of aesthetics that the Positivists approached tentatively, or simply refused to tackle. However, in England as well as on the Continent – not least in France – there was an undercurrent of aesthetic preoccupation that became increasingly strong as the 19th century drew towards tis close.

The opponents of Positivist procedures and thinking were anxious to demonstrate that determinism and the Positivist predilection for counting, weighing, and measuring, were inapplicable to the world of the mind and, by inference, also to the world of art and criticism. They pointed out that Positivst science had made little or no progress as far as man's knowledge of himself was concerned.

Some of those counter-tendencies are important in their own right. Thus *l'art pour l'art* is a challenge to the hegemony of science. But Baudelaire, one of the foremost representatives of the art for art's sake movement, is also relevant for Imagism and the Imagists because of his theory of *correspondances* between the arts. Another, later, development is Symbolism, which, in its conception of reality and the possibility of conveying an impression of it, anticipates Imagist theory and practice.

And, no less interesting, there were individual critics who, like Ruskin, concentrated their attacks on one aspect of the late Victorian ideals, or who, like the German philosopher Theodor Lipps, established a carefully elaborated theory of art that owed nothing to Positivist philosophy. Finally, and most important for the subject of this book, there was a rich crop of poetical theory and criticism of poetry written by French authors who were frequently both poets and critics. There is no late 19th century English equivalent to such speculations; contemporary English tendencies were mostly scientific, social, or intellectual [1].

The French theories came to be very influential in England, especially after the turn of the century. Hulme's friend Fletcher began to study French in 1903, and in his poetry as well as in his criticism he worked as a significant cross-Channel link in the first decade of the 20th century. The work of those French writers was not a function of Positivist thinking: it is not only that they were opposed to Positivism, it is also that they worked on entirely different premises. By liberating poetry from the Positivist straitjacket they were instrumental in establishing a more just balance between science and poetry and reinstating poetry in a more respected position than the Positivists had been willing to grant it.

L'art pour l'art

"Voir, sentir, exprimer, tout l'art est là," said Goncourt[2]. Art should be neither didactic, nor true, nor good, and it was to take no interest in ordinary morality. The art for art's sake movement did not arise in the latter half of the 19th century as a protest movement against Positivism. Actually, the idea goes back to the middle of the 18th century, when the German philosopher Alexander Gottlieb Baumgarten coined the term *aesthetics* to characterize the science of sensation and the Beautiful itself (*Aesthetica*, 1750-58). And around the turn of the 19th century, the Romanticists attacked social and moral art and considered industrialism the Beast in Revelations[3].

In England, the Pre-Raphaelites, who, like Hulme and the other Imagists, sought their ideals in pre-Renaissance art, were the first group of artists that took an interest in the art for art's sake movement. The Pre-Raphaelite Brotherhood was established in 1848, and one of its doctrines was that art was an ideal beyond nature and life; it was its own kind of thing, which made it inimical to Positivism. The point for the artist was to find an ideal world that is not subjected to reality, ie nature. Poe talked about "the poem *per se*", and Baudelaire, who translated Poe, used the formulation "*la poésie pure*", without, however, supporting the statement with any coherent theory. The artists were more articulate in their criticism of current values than in the establishment of a theoretical basis. Consequently, in their treatment, art became revelatory rather than imitative, a fact which made the movement interesting to the Imagists.

A central point for the art for art's sake artists was their assumption of the sisterhood of the arts. Baudelaire, who is an important figure in this respect, talked about images and symbols as being "*renouvelés par le subtil réseau des correspondances*". It was not only a correspondence between heaven and earth, for the young Baudelaire was at least as interested in painting as in literature[4], and his *Petits poèmes en prose* was an attempt to shape a musical prose without rhyme. French poets were advised to seek inspiration and support in the plastic arts, and several of the poets were familiar with the techniques of other arts.

The Imagists were enthusiastic about the idea of the sisterhood of the arts. Thus Hulme was captivated by what he saw as the geometrical construction of Cezanne's paintings, and the sculptures of his friend Gaudier-Brzeska had a great fascination for him. He frequently quotes with approval theoretical statements made by that sculptor of Franco-Polish extraction.

The art for art's sake movement prided itself on its exclusivity. It was essentially anti-democratic, a fact that won Hulme's warm support. By its opponents it was accused of being immoral because it maintained that art that depicts evil persons or sordid events can very well be great art. The deliberate dandyism of its French exponents – eg Baudelaire's explicit disgust of his own age as manifested in his *Spleen de Paris* (1869) – did not exactly make it popular with the late Victorian bourgeoisie. What *can* be said, however, is that it cultivated a narrow view of art, an ivory tower attitude to the surrounding world – an attitude that found considerable support with the Imagists.

THEODOR LIPPS

The German philosopher Theodor Lipps is included in this book because his speculations on 'geometrical art' were a source of inspiration to Hulme, who pays tribute to him on several occasions. Lipps wrote extensively on aesthetics, psychology, and philosophy, His *Raumästetik und geometrisch-optische Täuschungen* was published in 1897. That book, like the others that Lipps wrote, is anti-Positivist in its general tendency as well as in its details: the definitions it establishes are vague and elusive, the concepts he introduces are comprehensive and often muddled and amply provided with metaphysical overtones. In *Raumästetik* he introduces something he calls *free forms,* which are forms whose beauty is independent of an imagined placing in a given natural context. What characterizes beautiful geometrical forms is intelligibility, immanent regularity, and freedom – those terms being largely synonymous in Lipps' usage. It is an obvious weakness that Lipps does not define the concept of beauty; nor does he substantiate his claim that regularity is synonymous with beauty. All that he says is that when we 'feel' that what is geometrical is beautiful, there is no need for us to investigate the basis of that feeling[5].

Lipps' book is richly illustrated with lines, squares, circles, etc, which are commented on with considerable verbosity. The German philosopher reads certain 'regularities' into such forms – arbitrary 'laws' deduced from his Bergson-like postulate that there is in all figures an inherent activity (*Tätigkeit*). The rules he establishes are vitiated by the relativity of his terminology: smaller, bigger, more powerful, etc., and those labels seem to operate only in conjunction with their opposites. The message of the book is debilitated by the complete absence of any reference to a concrete work of art.

Another aspect of Lipps' thinking that is of relevance to Hulme and the Imagists is his claim that art is not imitative[6]. Art does not render reality or something that exists in reality, but something that is freely shaped on the analogy of reality.

John Ruskin

From the 1850s and onwards, Ruskin launched a series of violent attacks on capitalist economy. He claims that modern economists had misunderstood the term economy: it does not mean saving money, it means the administration of a house. In *Unto this Last* (the title is a quotation from Matthew XX, 14), he propagated a simple thesis, viz. that human beings cannot be considered as mere economic units, and he spoke up on behalf of 'social affections'. The good life can only be lived in a good society, and that is not one where man is treated as an animated machine.

Fors Clavigera with the subtitle *Letters to the Workmen and Labourers of Great Britain* (1871-1878) continues Ruskin's savage attacks on capitalist economy. He contrasts the sordid experience of many working-class people with the beauty and edification he found in art.

It was his enthusiasm for the paintings of Turner (whose executor he became) that made Ruskin a critic of art. The first volume of his impressive work *Modern Painters* was published in 1843, when he was in his middle thirties, and successive volumes followed until 1860. The sympathies and antipathies expressed in that work stayed with Ruskin for the rest of his life: he found Turner's work greatly superior to those of the old Dutch masters, he loved Renaissance painting, and he detested Renaissance architecture, which he found mediocre compared to Gothic architecture.

Ruskin's criticism was essentially moral: all education must be "moral first, intellectual secondarily", and it was his firm belief that "the arts can never be right themselves, unless their motive is right"[7]. In his criticism of art he deals exclusively with painting and architecture. Good art can be created only by good men, and his evaluation of works of art is based partly on the response they awake in him[8]. But at the same time he places the individual work in a huge context: just as the artist is a product of the social conditions of the age in which he lives, the work should be studied in relation to its time and – a suggestion reminiscent of Baudelaire's correspondences – be connected with the products of other arts.

Ruskin cultivates beauty as the supreme good. He never defines it, but illustrates it amply. He maintains that beauty is more important than life itself, and he wants to open people's eyes to the beauty of art – not least the English middle class, who had become all too philistine in their outlook. Matthew Arnold complained that "genius is too busy with him, intelligence not busy enough". His style is a mixture of the pithy formulation – he is the father of the expression 'the pathetic fallacy' – and the associational tangent. He was not the builder of a closely reasoned theory, and he concentrated his anti-Positivist attitude in repeated attacks on "the modern *soi-disant* science of political economy[9]. But Marcel Proust paid tribute to him for the inspiration he had provided.

FRENCH INFLUENCE

In the two decades surrounding the turn of the century, French culture and literature enjoyed enormous prestige in England. The influence is felt as early as the 1870s, when English poets borrowed material as well as stanza forms from beyond the Channel. Rimbaud became known to an English public in 1886 (although his poetry dates from the early 1870s). 1886 was also the year when Jules Laforgue wrote one of his seminal works, and in which Kahn published an essay on *vers libre*. Pater and Swinburne were instrumental in propagating the theory of art for art's sake on English soil, and there were some French poets and critics who concentrated on the literary work (especially the poem), partly drawing far-reaching conclusions in continuation of the art for art's sake dictum, partly digging deeper and discussing genuinely fundamental problems: if the work of art is its own end, creating a world of its own – Baumgarten had talked about *novus mundus* – how did it come into being, and what was its status? Laforgue praises Baudelaire for the 'bored uselessness' (*inutilité ennuyée*) of his *Fleurs du mal* in an age when most other people are working hard[10].

MIMESIS

The first stumbling block in discussions of the theory of poetry was mimesis. For if the poets did not accept the conventional scientific view of reality, why then imitate it? It was not so much the Platonic objection about the particular being an imperfect imitation of an imitation that appealed to them, it was rather that even a selctive abstraction was felt to be untrue. Reality could and should be viewed creatively.

As early as in 1847, Gautier wrote that "the mere imitation of nature cannot be the end of the artist"[11], and Baudelaire said that "poetry is that in which there is more of reality, it is that which is not completely true in *an other world*"[12] (his italics). In those statements there is much that foreshadows the position of Hulme and the Imagists. Hulme, too, was opposed to the idea that a poem should moralize or be useful. However, his starting-point was the existing world, and what he wanted to create was not a new – imaginary – world, but a new way of looking at 'our' world. He objected to the monolopy of science with regard to the description of reality, and he was satisfied that an equally true – perhaps even a more true – conception of reality could be conveyed by the striking image.

Creation. Ribot

A second point that engaged the French critics was the creation of the work of art. The *Essai sur l'imagination créatrice* by Théodule Ribot, who was professor of comparative experimental psychology at the Collège de France, appeared in 1900. Ribot is of crucial importance for Hulme and the Imagists in that he furnishes a significant part of the theoretical foundation of their practice.

As Ribot sees it, creation is a stepwise progression, the starting-point of which is an emotional factor[13]. In the next stage, pictures are called forth, and they objectify themselves in a form[14], which, in the case of literature, is the linguistic garb. Already at this early stage we see clearly the anti-Positivist tendency: creation is not an intellectual process, and pictures seem to crop up spontaneously without the conscious mediation of the artist. Of course, the Positivists had taken no interest at all in the problem of poetic creation.

The distinguishing feature of the creative imagination, says Ribot, is that it works in terms of analogies: in the moment of creation, the thought proceeds by analogies. From a subjectively seen or sensed similarity, an objective identity is inferred. Once the process has been completed, the resulting image obtains the same value as an actually existing connection between the two items that make up the analogy[15].

Even though Ribot's assumptions are hypotheses, they could not but be pleasing to the Imagists' ears. His claim that the image that is the result of the creative process has the same value as an actually existing connection between the two items had far-reaching consequences: the picture acquires truth status, the reader has his eyes opened, has acquired new insight, and has had his world view changed, be it ever so slightly. The assumption is that the creative artist is capable of making an impact on the reader's conception of *natura naturata* in that items of it, when seen through the poet's eyes and conveyed in his words, acquire fresh status and establish hitherto unrealized relationships. Imagist manifestos never tire of stressing the necessity of 'seeing things as they are', the implication being 'not necessarily seeing them as they are conventionally, ie by the Positivists, taken to be'. And Ribot had great confidence in the mind's capacity to produce images: he operates with a concept that he calls *spontanité*, which causes images to assemble in ever new combinations. The word remains unexplained, but, like the whole of Ribot's system, is not devoid of some cogency. The Imagists adopted the idea; they were convinced that an image could 'spontaneously' generate others in the writing process.

Gourmont

In the issue of March 16, 1914 of *The Egoist*[16], Aldington says that many young English writers who are interested in the theory of literature and art find Rémy de Gourmont the most fascinating artist now living in France, an opinion which is whole-heartedly endorsed by Aldington himself. Aldington also paid tribute to Gourmont in an obituary of the French author and critic, who died in 1915[17].

The interest of Gourmont on the part of Aldington and the Imagists is understandable. It was not his novels that captivated them, but his literary theories and poetical practice. *Le Problème du Style*, of which the preface was written in 1902, is a fascinating analysis of the use and function of imagery in poetry. The main thesis of the book is that there exists an intimate relationship between style and sensibility[18]. Again and again Gourmont stresses *vision* and *émotion* as the twin sources of style. He states, with pretended surprise, that, 200 years after Locke, it is still necessary to emphasize the fact that sensation is the basis of everything[19]. A person's sensation, or seeing, may provide him with a visual memory, a reservoir on which his imagination can draw so as to form new and never-ending combinations. A poet must possess that kind of memory, for, without it, it is impossible to produce style, or, altogether, a work of art[20]. Wordsworth would have nodded approval. Style is visual memory plus a talent for metaphor, combined in variable proportions with emotive memory and obscure contributions from the senses[21].

If an author sees and hears and feels, he is bound to be able to write[22]. Seeing is the first stage in the creative process, but imagination is richer than the largely passive memory because it is able to work with the material that memory provides it with: to imagine is to associate images and fragments of images – it is never to create. Thus, imagination becomes a kind of mechanical organizer, in function much like Coleridge's fancy.

So, literature does contain a mimetic element. Gourmont is at pains to underline that all imaginative literature is based on reality, as is the case with science[23]. But the difference is that literature recasts when imitating. Gourmont goes so far as to assert that reality in itself has no meaning – every detail that is 'merely real' is useless. When you particularize, you should not accumulate the same facts as a zoologist would do in his description of an animal. Like Dr Johnson, Gourmont warns the poet against the inane counting of the streaks of the tulip.

No modern theorist would need to be ashamed of Gourmont's explanation of metaphor: in a metaphor there are not two ideas (*dessins*) symmetrically put on top of one another, but a visually absurd and artistically admirable merging of a double and *trouble* (ie not limpid) sense impression[24]. Whereas similes are liable to be transferred to pictorial representation – and Gourmont claims that the result will be geometrical art – because they are separable, that process is impossible in the case of metaphors[25].

However, to Gourmont, there is something even more sophisticated than metaphor, and that is the device he calls *l'art suprême*. He instances a basilica that has been 'flayed' so as to present to the beholder's eyes only its bones and ridges: the underlying image will be that of a whale, the two complementary images having been merged into a third that is quite unexpected. That to Gourmont is ' the supreme art' because the *tertium comparationis* is not explicitly mentioned, the point being that it would be needless[26]. Hulme has several poems exemplifying that 'supreme art', where a deconstructionist reading would reveal surprising differences from what the poem purported to be about.

There are striking similarities between Gourmont's poems and Hulme's. Most of the Frenchman's poems are short, consisting of no more than one image. Very few of them are narrative, the emphasis being on an image – of water, air, dryness, wetness, the life cycle of plants, and, above all, gems and flowers of all imaginable kinds and colours. The formal characteristics of the poems are occasional rhymes and, frequently, a stanzaic structure.

Gourmont's poems differ from Hulme's in that a dominant theme is love, many poems being love scenes disguised as descriptions of exotic flowers. A discreet but elegant homage is paid to woman and her body, and a veiled sexuality pervades the poems. That is true of some of Hulme's poems, too, but generally speaking, his range of themes is wider than the Frenchman's.

Gourmont called his poems *Divertissements*, which is remarkable in the light of the fact that the tone is nostalgic and wistful. The narrator, who plays an active part in the majority of the poems, is grave and prone to sadness, as if shaking his head in despair at the impossibility of ever having his love reciprocated.

Laforgue

The *Mélanges posthumes* of Jules Laforgue was published posthumously in 1903 (he died in 1887, aged 27). It is a miscellaneous collection of prose pieces, often little more than sketches. His style is verbose and permeated with imagery. The syntax is a mixture of short sentences, often with the verb in the infinite form, and long, convoluted concatenations of words.

The title of the section called *Paysages et impressions* is very appropriate. It consists mainly of short descriptions full of anthropomorphous images with an abundance of sounds, colours, and personifications (but no classical allusions). The landscape and town scenes are treated as organisms, and observations tumble over each other, each of them provided with an image, none of them being elaborated in any detail. Such human beings as appear are there simply in the capacity of stage properties, not as agents. The narrator does not address anybody, indeed he says that he has been walking in the streets of Paris for days without speaking to anyone[27].

Laforgue's essays are sprinkled with personal comments of a theoretical kind. Thus, in the notes on Rimbaud, we read that a poem is not necessarily an emotion that the poet conveys in the form it was conceived before it was written down. Digressions on the way are permissible if the poet makes a real find[28]. It is remarks like those which seem to support the assertion that 'the poem writes itself'.

In a long essay[29], Laforgue pays a warm and enthusiastic tribute to Impressionist painting. In the context of this book it is interesting to note that he admired its *réalité décomposée*. He also comments on the Impressionists' use of form: they achieved formal excellence not by design and outline, but exclusively by the vibrations and contrasts of colours. The Baudelairean *correspondance* is perceptible here, for the parallel with poetry is not far to seek: it is not a fixed and rigid metrical pattern that creates great poetry, but colourful images that succeed, and are contrasted to, each other. Laforgue compliments the Impressionists for replacing theoretical perspective by what he calls 'natural perspective': the eye of the Impressionist painter sees reality 'in the living atmosphere of the forms', a kind of reality that is decomposed and refracted by objects and living beings[30]. The straight line is boring, the ideal is the line broken a thousand times, *"pétillants d'écarts imprévus"* that deceive the eye and whip it onwards. Laforgue's comment on the broken line can be paralleled with a linguistic discourse which does not proceed in an unimaginative linear progression, but is 'broken' by striking images, which, however, only contribute to emphasizing the forward movement – dynamism again.

Laforgue wants to do away with official or ideal beauty: people should learn to see for themselves. And then, quite naturally, they will gravitate towards painters that fascinate them. Interestingly, such painters will be neither Greek nor Renaissance artists, but Egyptian and modern ones.

It was his use of imagery and his treatment of metre that made Laforgue and his poetry *the* sources of inspiration and the point of reference to the Imagists as well as, to a considerable extent, Eliot. Like the other adherents of the art for art's sake idea he detested the sordid world (*"le monde encrassé"*), and he claimed that his *"désespoir métaphysique"* had its origin in the reading of Schopenhauer.

Many of his poems have no titles and are not narrative but descriptive in a very restricted sense. A dominant theme is the contrast between the narrator's scarred soul and the unsympathetic outside world. The title of the collection *Les Complaintes* (1885) is symptomatic. Some of the poems are love poems, addressed to an unidentified 'you', whose outward appearance is sketchily described in laudatory or respectful terms. The poems are not located in time or place, and the main emphasis is on the description of the narrator's mood, which is one of spleen: he is sad and pensive, but at the same time also sedate and apathetic. It is a matter of discreet and asexual adoration at a distance. The reader is left with the impression that Laforgue may have written these poems as an attempt to scrutinize and lay bare the reactions of his own mind – or simply as a poetical exercise.

Laforgue's poems show a remarkable range of vocabulary taken from widely different fields. He has a partiality for words describing colours or shades of colours. He uses quite a number of rare or uncommon words, frequently such as are provided with classical overtones. However, it is in his use of images that he is a genuine innovator. Admittedly, some of them are familiar ones: "If I die, harvested by life, cut down by the scythe of time…"[31]. But many images are original and bold: "the street falls asleep like an endless complaint"[32], "gliding like a suffering straw I would walk away from you towards a great gulf"[33], " my love is deep as a deserted sea, serious as a summer evening"[34]. His images are similes rather than metaphors, and one idea may prompt comparisons from widely different areas. Glances vibrate "like uncorporeal seraphs, the agile movements of dancing street performers, and undulating clear-cheeked swans' necks in a pond." Some of them are profoundly tragic. The narrator's love is "made of amber, jade and ivory, and is beautiful as the milk of the river Lethe"[35], in which the mention of the precious items of the former half is undercut by the reference to forgetfulness in the second.

Laforgue was on friedly terms with Gustave Kahn, one of the theorists of *vers libre*. Therefore, it is not surprising that Laforgue should experiment with poetical form. Most of his poetry is stanzaic, but both the stanzas and the lines are of unequal length. Usually the line coincides with speech rhythm; rhymes do occur, but they are not arranged in any kind of pattern, and sometimes the same word is used as a recurrent rhyme. The poems are meant to be read aloud, or perhpas rather chanted: they are incantations. The collection *L'Imitation de Notre-Dame de la Lune* , which was published in 1886, is, also from a formal point of view, a significant experiment.

CHAPTER SIX

BREAKTHROUGH OF THE ANTI-POSITIVISTS

PLANCK

Around the turn of the 19th century, the rebellion against the theory and practice of Positivism had become manifest and widespread. New angles of approach were felt to be indispensable, and the title of one of the literary periodicals from 1907, *New Age*, is symptomatic.

The interesting thing is that doubts were beginning to be raised within one of the bastions of Positivism, viz. science. The German physicist Max Planck (1858-1947) said in *The Unity of the Physical World Picture* (1908-1909) that "the most important feature of all scientific research is a demand for a *constant* world picture independent of all evolutions in time and among human beings"[1] (his italics). But, as Hamlet would have said, there is the rub. For though he advocated "the emancipation of science from anthropomorphic elements not from the creative mind as such, but from the *individuality* of the creative mind"[2] (his italics), Planck had to admit that physicists daily form generalizations "when making conclusions going beyond direct observation which can never be tested by human observation"[3]. In other words, a human or subjective element can never be excluded. Henri Poincaré, the French mathematician (1854-1912) is quoted as saying that science always presupposes a duality between the object known and the mind that knows, ie consciousness is separate from its object. That is eminently illustrated in Imagist poetry, where a hidden or discreet narrator observes and describes.

Max Planck was convinced of the existence of what he called *das Reale*, ie "a constancy that is independent of every human, especially every intellectual, individuality"[4]. He maintained the idea of constancy as a kind of defensive postulate, but he was also aware that "das Reale" was ungraspable by human investigation and understanding.

"Nature loves to hide," said Heraclitus, and, as Philip Wheelwright has pointed out, "reality is ultimately problematic; trying to grasp and formulate it, one risks fragmentizing it. There is more than meets the eye. We cannot hope to be perfectly right, but, from time to time, we can change ways of being wrong"[5].

Einstein

The vulnerability of the idea of constancy had been demonstrated by Einstein (1879-1955), who, as early as in 1895, had pointed out some aspects of the quality of light that disturbed the current world picture. And in 1905, he presented his theory of relativity, which was a challenge to the Olympic figure of classical physics, Newton. To begin with, the reception was sceptical: surely those theories were incompatible with common sense and would lead to absurd consequences? But in 1915, Einstein's theory proved superior to Newton's because, for the first time, an irregularity in the orbit of the planet Mercury was accounted for – an irregularity that had been known to observation since 1879.

Reality to Einstein is planned, and physics is a means to understand that plan. "God does not throw dice," as he said in his famous answer to Bohr, who had maintained the impossibility of getting to know anything about reality *an sich*. Be that as it may, God was a word that the Positivists avoided, and Bohr's and Einstein's achievements heralded a new world picture. Thus Bohr pointed out that the result of a physical experiment is not only determined by physical factors; it also depends on the – subjectively arranged – conditions under which the experiment is carried out.

And of course the concept of reality changed further when, soon after the turn of the century, physicists began to explore the world of atoms. The questions that posed themselves more and more urgently were these: is there such a thing as 'ultimate reality'? Can we ever hope to get at the *Ding an sich?* And – if so – is the human thought capable of comprehending it, and is the human language able to render it in plain words, or can it only be described metaphorically? Many people, including scientists, were beginning to suspect what Wittgenstein was to formulate succinctly in his *Tractatus*[6]: "At the basis of the whole modern view of the world lies the illusion that the so-called laws of nature are the explanation of natural phenomena"

The Humanities

After the turn of the century, the intellectual movement is away from science, whose concept of truth is increasingly being questioned. Within philosophy, there is a search for non-logical faculties of cognition. Hulme turned to religion as a protest against the Positivists' atheism and materialism.

Equally, there was a demand for a novel departure within literature, which had been characterized by too much of what Pound called "Tennysonianisms of speech"[7]. On the whole, the first decade of the 20th century sees a revolution in many areas: Einstein's theory of relativity, Freud's attempt to found a 'science of the mind' by using introspection, a procedure that the late 19th century scientists disdained because they considered it highly suspicious, even dangerous; Freud's interpretation of dreams (1900), Lenin's theories about the structures of a Marxist party (*What Should Be Done?* (1902)), Picasso's picture *Les Demoiselles d'Avignon* (1907), which heralds Cubism – all of them make the first ten years of the 20th century a watershed in western civilization.

The arts had it out with Positivism in an effort to justify the aesthetic experience and restore it to its pristine health. Once more, French influence was clearly perceptible: it is characteristic of late 19th century French literary criticism and philosophy that they concentrate on the form of the work of art and the role of the imagination in the creative act. The idea of the sisterhood of the arts was enthusiastically embraced. In his *Art poétique* (1871-73) Verlaine had stated that the point was to create "de la musique avant toute chose", and one of Hulme's best friends was the sculptor Gaudier-Brzeska, whose works he admired because they were 'geometrical' and non-representative. His works, like those of another friend of Hulme's, Jacob Epstein, represent a rugged breakaway from the school of Rodin.

The artists' shared intention was to give alternative visions of reality from that provided by Positivist science. The Impressionist painters do not fill their canvasses with precisely observed details. The pictures dissolve and blur photographic likeness and reveal what a fleeting glance may discover, and their main concern is the play of light upon objects – light is the main character of a picture, to speak with Monet. Impressionist painting is a pictorial illustration of Mallarmé's words: "To name an object is to sacrifice three quarters of that enjoyment of the poem which comes from the guessing bit by bit. To *suggest* - that is our dream".

Wagner wrote the libretti of his own operas, and Debussy transferred Mallarmé's words to music that had an allusive vagueness and used harmonies that were mellifluous in a different way from eg Tschaikovsky's. Debussy used tone in the same way as the Impressionist painters used light. Musical impressionism – the term used to characterize Debussy's music – gathered momentum after Debussy returned to Paris from Rome in 1887. The Symbolists were very interested in music.

Symbolism

Symbolism in literature, like Impressionism in painting and music, originated with a group of artists in Paris. The word symbolism was used by Moréas in 1886. Basically, Symbolism is a quest for unity, an attempt to create meaning and coherence in an apparently meaningless and fluctuating world. In France, it was a reaction against the precision and objectivity of the poets who called themselves *Parnassiens*.

It was Arthur Symons' book *The Symbolist Movement in Literature* that introduced Symbolism to an English audience. The book is from 1899, but some germs of Symbolism may be found in Poe's criticism of Romantic looseness and his discussion of indefiniteness[8]. Symons' book is a collection of essays on late 19th century French poets. Very early in the book the author characterizes Symbolism as an "approximate, but arbitrary expression for an unseen reality"[9], a thought he returns to later when he talks about "the eternal correspondence between the visible and the invisible universe"[10]. Unfortunately, the book sheds virtually no light on how the Symbolists actually use the tools of their trade.

The Symbolists refused to accept the assumption that was taken for granted by many Positivist writers, viz. that there is a one-to-one correspondence between a word and its referent. The point about a symbol is that can communicate even in a context where such a correspondence does not exist. As Carlyle put it: in a symbol there is concealment, and yet revelation[11]. Hence the Symbolists' predilection for suggestion and evocation: they found that since feelings are so different, they cannot be adequately rendered in the conventional literary language. Accordingly, their efforts were directed towards finding images possessing a personal flavour – each poet would have to invent his own language, and such idiosyncratic formulations were supposed to 'symbolize' the poet's emotion. Symbolist poets claimed that 'the world' only comes into existence when a poet has seen it 'significantly'[12]. In a proud boast, Symons calls Symbolism "an establishing of the links that hold the world together"[13].

Symbolism contained elements that were bound to appeal immediately to Hulme and the Imagists. The Symbolist concern for the idiosyncratic use of language and the attempt to draw from striking and unconventional images an effect that might put across the poet's vision and give the reader glimpses of insight and concomitant thrills of pleasure, were adopted whole-heartedly by the Imagists. And, like their Symbolist predecessors, the Imagists were convinced that art should be dissociated from morality and from social repsonsibility.

However, the differences between the two schools of poetry are at least as significant as the similarities. The Symbolists saw subtle affinities between the material and the spiritual worlds. And they put a question mark off the status and function of the objective world. The Imagists, on the contrary, had their feet firmly planted on the ground in that they concentrated on the image itself rather than on a possible ultimate reality hidden behind it. They wanted to create, and open their readers' eyes to, a new relation between language and the world[14]. The Symbolists saw symbols everywhere, whereas to the Imagists the images they used were not keys to the solution of the riddles of the univese..

Matters are further complicated by the fact that the words 'symbol' and 'Symbolism' are used in three different senses by Hulme's immediate predecessors and contemporaries: first, as a vague synonym for poetic imagery (Symons is often to blame on this point); secondly, referring to a specific device exploited in poetry, that which Jules Lemaître called "une comparaison prolongée dont on ne nous donne que le second terme"[15]: and, thirdly, as a technical term for a philosophy, viz. the practice of giving a symbolic character to objects or acts.

CHAPTER SEVEN

INDEBTEDNESS

INTRODUCTION

The victory of the 'rebels' over Positivism dealt with in the previous chapter did not imply that all that Positivism had stood for had to go by the board. Some of the questions they debated – eg what is reality, and is there an adequate way of describing it? – had not originally been raised by the Positivists and were far too comprehensive and complicated to have been given a definite and satisfactory answer. And the methods they had adopted – observation, analysis, categorization – could of course be used for other purposes than those cultivated by the Positivists. Finally, some of the Positivist ideas seemed to be in tune with the mental climate of the first decades of the 20th century so that, also by then, they appeared to be obviously true. Dynamism is a case in point.

Reality continued to be a sticking-point also to the post-Positivists. Philosophers and scientists increasingly tended to side with the dictum of the 18th century philosopher David Hume (1711-1776) to the effect that in cases of 'matter of fact' we will never get beyond our sense impressions, which are the starting-point. Nor is it possible to establish any connection between sense impressions: there is only 'immediate awareness'. David Hume's assertions were of crucial significance to the Imagists, for what they imply is that 'a coherent world' is a figment of our brain, but, unlike David Hume, they thought that reality *can* be comprehended, albeit only in bits and pieces. That is what the Imagists tried to do in their short poems, which often consisted of only one image that illuminated one aspect of reality and conveyed 'an immediate awareness'.

WITTGENSTEIN

The idea of the significance of the image was supported by the questioning of the potentialities of language – a point that was to be developed by Wittgenstein in his *Tractatus* (1921): since it is impossible to *say* something about the really important matters, it is far better to *show* than to *tell*. Meaning is not embedded in the words, meaning is produced by the use we make of words. That statement is a blow to any rigid definition of reality. Wittgenstein's assumptions might very well have been included in an Imagist manifesto (if he had not been a decade late!), as could his theory, inspired by David Hume, that the world is a collection of discrete facts. The Imagists showed instead of saying, and – like Wittgenstein – they used analogies to put their message across.

Like the Positivists, their successors in the first decades of the 20th century excluded the idea of the Godhead from their speculations (as did Wittgenstein). It is characteristic that Imagist poetry does not contain interpretations of life; what it does give is an idiosyncratic representation of the world we live in – very much in tune with Wittgenstein's matter of fact tackling of linguistic issues.

Dynamism and Categorization

Post-Positivists stood on the shoulders of their predecessors in several respects. The Positivist preoccupation with dynamism, energy and movement was carried on with great enthusiasm by their early 20th century successors. Dynamism was not a Positivist invention. Heraclitus (c. 540 – 480 b.C.) held that 'all things are in a state of flux' (panta rhei), and that the essential stuff of the universe is pure fire. Mme Curie's discovery, in 1898, of radium, which can transform itself into energy, corroborated what the Positivists had maintained, viz. that energy is a force of nature. Also researchers' predilection for categorizing and compartmentalizing their findings survived Positivism.

The tendencies were not always found in a state of pure cultivation in one person or movement, and they always went hand in hand with more modern thinking. Thus *vers libre* was given its name because, following the dynamism of the speech rhythm, it was 'liberated', set against the background of more traditional metre. There were actually some French critics who referred to it as *vers libéré*, rather than *vers libre*. Of course, 'free verse' was also evidence of the current interest in the form of the object.

Using the analytical practices of Positivism, Freud divided the human being, which was the object of his analysis, into a conscious and an unconscious part, and he disputed the monopoly of consciousness to control behaviour. Freud was not the only one who used the individual as his object of analysis. Actually Comte had taken some preliminary steps, but his interest was in the individual as a member of society. In *Principles of Psychology* (1890), William James declared that introspection is the method of scientific psychology. He opined that consciousness, which he characterized as a stream, is a tool for the appropriate development of man's social life.

Bergson

Beneath the metaphysical fogginess of much of Bergson's thinking runs an undercurrent of Positivist dynamism and an urge to channel that dynamism into a system that ran counter to the explanations of natural science, yet claimed to have the same truth value as the Positivist system of ideas. He is relevant in the context of this book not only in his own right because his thinking combines rebellion against, and indebtedness to, the Positivists, but also, more specifically, because he exerted a profound influence on the Imagists and Hulme.

Bergson's philosophy is essentially dynamic, and most of his axioms can be subsumed under the headings of movement and energy. His anti-Positivism took various shapes. His *Évolution créatrice* (1907), which forms the cornerstone of his philosophy, and which, characteristically, uses a biological term in the title of a book on psychology, straddles biology, psychology, and metaphysics, and it consists of a series of unargued assumptions that are not rationally verifiable, but only graspable by empathy or intuition. Mechanism and finality were anathema to Bergson[1]; he rejected teleology, he was scared of the 'deterministic nightmare', and he refused to acknowledge the existence of a First Cause.

His works are a row of variations upon a very limited number of themes. He employs conventional philosophical concepts like matter, consciousness, and time, adding some new ones, like energy and intuition. But from the outset he tries to disarm criticism by saying that language as a medium is unreliable: it has been circumscribed by being used mainly for intellectual purposes. That is of course a smart trick, for it means that Bergson feels justified in desisting from any kind of precise defintion, which is regrettable, for not infrequently he gives new and idiosyncratic content to conventional philosophical concepts. Another reason that makes it difficult for the reader to arrive at a total comprehension is that the same term is used with different meanings that are not obviously related. So, more than once, the reader is excusably baffled.

Bergson postulates the existence of a current of creative energy that he calls *l'élan commun*. Thus he starts from what he acknowledges as a postulate, whereas the Positivists maintained that they 'asked nature', which made their findings incontrovertible. Like several of his contemporaries, Bergson conceived of consciousness as a current. The ontological status of the *élan* is obscure, it is a metaphysical entity whose origin its inventor does not even discuss. Individual beings are landmarks (*points de repère*) in this forward movement, which is greater than the individuals themselves.

The *élan* is also greater than matter: matter is a momentary stop in the push of the *élan*. However, it is unable to stop the current permanently. Here, in embryo, is one of the dichotomies which the Imagists and Hulmne returned to again and again, viz. the contrast between flux and stasis. They believed that, with his images, a poet can create a momentary stop in the current that was existence. The poetic image acquired an epiphany-like quality because it would momentarily initiate the reader into 'what things were really like'. At the same time, it was a resting-point in a world of confusion.

According to Bergson, the *élan*, by running through matter, confers freedom on it. Life is "un courant à travers la matière". The *élan* is also called pure will, and it is cognate with human consciousness, but what or whose volition is responsible for the forward movement remains obscure. Only one thing is certain: the will is not God's.

Anti-Positivist though he was, Bergson wanted to understand, and make intelligible, what reality actually is. Reality is a flux and cannot be grapsed by intelligence, but only by intuition, a point that Bergson substantiates by referring to the fact that many theories within physics have first been propunded as intuitions, but have later been proved rationally. Whereas intelligence proceeds mechanically, intuition proceeds organically. Intuition, which is not given even a tentaive definition, is not only "l'esprit même" - it is life in itself[2]. By the same token, Bergson operates with a 'fundamental Self', whose states are completely interpenetrative, and which can only be comprehended by an entirely different kind of knowing, viz. intuition. What this means is that Bergson's criteria of validity differ radically from those of the Positivists. Direct communicability is no longer an asset. In another leap of thought, Bergson claims that all the powers (*puissances*) of the body converge on action, which, in his idiolect, means a capacity to bring about changes in things[3]. But Bergson's idea of change is obscure: what is to be changed, along what lines is the change going to take place, and what is the goal? As we have seen, he rejects finality and teleology, but he also maintains that permanence is synonymous with worthlessness.

The mind's basic acticity is action, but the artist's prerogative is that he is excused from action. That status does not seem to impair the prestige of the artist, however. The thought is repeated *ad nauseam* by the Imagists, but the reader is left with a lurking suspicion that they do not really know what is means. None of them tries to get to grips with the statement.

In regard to time, Bergson's terminology is no less idiosyncratic: reality is a perpetual becoming. And Bergson introduces the concept of *durée*, which is the cornerstone in his reflections on time. 'Durée' is associated with movement.

But it is not simply the opposite of immobility. It is the continuation of the past and the active intervention of the past into the present. Movement is in principle indivisible, but 'durée' can be punctuated by action[4]. What Bergson seems to imply is that whereas *élan* is movement *per se*, *durée* is man's perception of the movement – an idea that would have seemed absurd to the Positivist scientists. Yet Bergson does not go so far as to discuss whether each individual has his or her own 'durée' even though human consciousness confers rhythm on the 'durée'.

In *Matière et Mémoire* (1900), Bergson introduces the concept of *image*, which is very nearly synonymous with 'that which can be the object of perception', ie a radically different meaning from Imagist usage, which is linguistically based. Matter, then, becomes the sum total of 'images'[5]. Perception starts from objects, it is not in the first place an activity of the human brain, a statement that would seem to need some kind of further explanation. The body is at one and the same time passively recording and actively intervening. Representation is the body's influence on other 'images', but the body is incapable of creating representation[6]. And yet the human consciousness is able to show a faithful copy of the immovable matter[7].

Bergson's intention was to show that just as the physical world is governed by laws, so is the human mind. He claimed to have established a coherent philosophical system, but it is a question whether a rational approach to his thinking is in any way rewarding, or indeed possible. He does not arrive at his results by acknowledged rules of argumentation, and there is no little confusion in his basic assumptions as well as in the details of his tenets. The uninitiated will unavoidably feel that he raises more questions than he answers, and much of his philosophy is so anti-science as to become mysticism.

BERGSON AND HULME

The two men met in Bologna in 1911, and for the rest of his life Hulme remained heavily indebted to the French philosopher. In the short essay *A Personal Impression of Bergson*, Hulme pays tribute to the Frenchman for "seeing things as they really are" – a favourite formulation with Hulme. The *Notes on Bergson* (1912) is said by Hulme himself to be "a personal confession". Bergson's achievement is to have found a new 'dialect'. The construction of the *Notes* is characteristic of Hulme's style (and perhaps of the way his brain worked): an idea is put forward, it is amply illustrated by wayward postulates and accompanied by numerous digressions, but never analysed in the proper sense of the word. In 1913, with the assistance of F.S.Flint, Hulme translated Bergson's *In-*

troduction à la Métaphysique. What appears from this translation, as well as from the bulk of Hulme's writing, is that he intuitively sensed and was partly won over by what the Frenchman was getting at.

Hulme was not without some admiration for the Positivists, and he was suspicious of Bergson's glorification of the irrational. But he found Bergson's theory of reality as a series of interpenetrated elements only graspable by intuition very much to the point. The comments that Bergson offers on the use and function of language left an idelible mark on Hulme and the Imagist movement: in ordinary perception we see things as conventional types, not as they 'really' are. Consequently, if he wants to convey what he sees, the artist will have to use images or analogies[8].

Form

The forms within painting and sculpture that the Positivists preferred were those handed down from the Renaissance. The post-Positivists continued the analytical interest, but included some new factors: they concentrated on non-representational forms. Cézanne was extolled for the 'geometrical' lines of his paintings, and Epstein's sculptures were widely admired on account of their non-representational character. Besides, and no less importantly, the post-Positivists were increasingly concerned with the reader's or beholder's reactions. Art was beginning to be looked upon as a personal matter between the work of art and the individual recipient.

Worringer

The mixture of Positivist preoccupation with lines and post-Positivist interest in the assessments of the individual is clearly illustrated in the German philosopher Wilhelm Worringer's book from 1908, *Abstraktion und Einfühlung*. The message of the book is in a nutshell that abstract, ie non-imitative, art is pleasing to the human soul. In the preface to *New Impression* (1948), the writer says that the influence exerted by the former book when it was first published was due to the fact that "a whole period was disposed for a radical reorientation of aesthetic value"[9].

The form of an object, says Worringer, is always its being-formed-by-me, by my inner activity[10]. He leaves imitation entirely out of consideration because the impulse to imitation "stands outside aesthetics proper and…its gratification has nothing to do with art"[11]. In the Renaissance, "truth to nature and art came to be looked upon as inseparable concepts". Once that fallacious inference had been drawn, it was a short step from regarding the real as the aim of art to looking upon imitation of the real as art[12]. It is Worringer's contention that "the primal artistic impulse has nothing to do with the rendering of nature. It seeks after pure abstraction as the only possibility of repose within the confusion and obscurity of the world picture, and creates out of itself, with instinctive necessity, geometrical construction"[13]. He cites historical evidence of his theory by describing the "psychic process of the evolution of art", according to which "the geometrical style must have stood at the beginning of all ornament, and the ornamental forms must gradually have developed out of it"[14]. And he plays his trump card: whenever we catch a glimpse of the artistic beginnings of the prehistoric ages of Europe and Egypt, "we find the assumption corroborated that art does not begin with naturalistic constructs, but with ornamental-abstract ones"[15].

In the preoccupation with abstraction. Worringer sees a fundamental illustration of man's relationship with *natura naturata:* "The simple line and its development in purely geometrical regularity was bound to offer the greatest possibility of happiness to the man disquieted by the obscurity and entanglement of phenomena"[16]. And later in the book he points out that "the point of departure for the impulse to artistic creation" is "the urge…to create resting-points, opportunities for repose" in the face of the bewildering and disquieting mutations of the phenomena of the outer world.

The reader's interests are foregrounded, and geometrical art is held to be mentally healthy. It is entirely in accordance with the anti-Positivist stance of Worringer and others that they claim priority for the reactions and assessments of the ego. A line may be drawn form Worringer's criticism to Eliot's theory of the 'objective correlative' (approaches to which are apparent in Hulme's writings): there, too, the reader's response is of paramount importance. Also Worringer's statements about 'resting-places' are forerunners of later developments: the Imagists and Hulme claimed that with their images they froze reality for an instant, thus creating stasis (and rest) in the flux.

That Hulme was familiar with the ideas contained in *Einfühlung* appears in a letter he wrote about it. "It simply means 'feeling oneself into the object' (sich fühlen ein). We 'feel ourselves' in mere lines, for example, ourselves moving along the line so that if the motion would be agreeable, we call the line beautiful – most generally, an explanation of the process by which it becomes possible to give to physical things in art, line, colour, etc., names which are appropriate to the mental states". But as a matter of fact, he is not unequivocally positive – to him the idea smacked of sentimentality, and he ends the letter with a disclaimer: "This is very confused…"[17].

Once more it will be seen how the theoretical substratum of Imagist theory and practice to a large extent was inspired from abroad – Bergson, Lipps, Worringer, Ribot, to name a few examples.

VERS LIBRE

The same goes for another seminal theory that was widely acclaimed in the early years of the 20th century, viz. the *vers libre* tradition. It was inspired by the reflections of the Frenchman Gustave Kahn, and it was related to the contemporary preoccupation with form. It was based on the idea that poetry is not expected to observe formal criteria imposed from outside the work itself, and it is another illustration of the tension between the interest in form in the abstract and the inherited Positivist dynamism.

In 1886, Laforgue translated Whitman's *Leaves of Grass*, which inspired him to work with a more free form of verse[18]. He liberated himself from the stanzaic structure in order to convey a sensation of strict truth "with the greatest possible sharpness and the largest amount of personal accent"[19]. Kahn said later that he had been toying with the same idea from approximately the same time. In his *Premiers Poèmes précédés d'une étude sur le vers libre* from 1897, we read: "I had for a long time within myself been trying to find a personal rhythm which would confer on my poems the *allure* and the *accent* that I considered indispensable"[20]. Much of the *Étude* was repeated verbatim in his book *Le vers libre*, which came out in 1912.

Kahn applies a biological evolutionary model to poetry: just like morals and fashions, poetic forms develop and die[21]. He is convinced that a change is needed within poetry, and for him the change is one of form rather than content. He attacks the rigidity of the alexandrine, but makes light of the fact that the alexandrine had made use of the *rejet* as well as of the *enjambement*. Following the prevalent fashion of *correspondances* he turns to music, where he finds a form that is at the same time *fluide* and *précise*[22].

Those terms, fluidity combined with precision, and with a personal accent of strict truth, are some of the key concepts of Kahn's theory of free verse. What happened 'ten years ago', he says, was that poets found it futile and frustrating to subject themselves to rules of whose weakness they were clearly aware. Modern poets want to express a more complex thought that cannot be circumscribed by the old forms[23]. His assumption, then, is that a new content requires a new form. He defines the unit of the verse – and with 'verse' he seems to refer to a line as well as to a stranza, though he also sometimes uses the word *strophe* – as "the shortest possible fragment showing a stop in the voice and in the meaning"[24]. Formerly, poetry was distinguished from prose thanks to "a certain arrangement". But the new poetry is distinguished from prose by music[25]: poetry should sing – if it does not, it is not poetry[26].

In order to bring *voix* and *sens* together, Kahn recommends other kinds of rhyme than end-rhyme, eg alliteration of related consonants and assonance of similar vowels. It is not that he proscribes the use of rhyme, what he would like to avoid is "the beat of the cymbal at the end of the verse"[27], and he is prepared to admit internal rhymes in cases where the rhythm invites them[28]. The overall idea is that the rhythm should be faithful to the sense, not to the symmetry[29]. Accordingly, each poet may conceive within himself his original line, or his original stanza[30], which may be a further reason why the result was called 'free verse'.

Not unexpectedly, Kahn refuses to codify any particular stanza form. It is all a matter of what he calls "the accent of impulse"[31] – dynamism again! The new symmetry that is thus achieved becomes more complicated than the traditional one because it will be a question of mobile rhymes and assonances[32]. Kahn does not want to establish a prosody: we do not need one right now, and anyway it is only required for those who insist on clinging to tradition[33]. Instead of prosody and poetics, he advocates personal reflections on technique[34], one more reason why 'free' is an appropriate designation for that kind of verse.

Kahn is very preoccupied with the total effect of the line and the stanza, and even if he is pretty skimpy about the subjects that poetry might suitably deal with, that does not mean that he entirely ignores the content of poetry. The poet's starting-point is himself, and he transposes all the facts that he knows and the emotions that he feels on to the intellectual field[35]. So, poetry is not just the gushing forth of idiosyncratic feelings. For such transposition, metaphors are necessary[36], and he quotes with approval the following words by Gautier: "Je vois le monde extérieur, et j'écris des métaphores qui se suivent"[37]. Kahn is fascinated by the idea that metaphors are able to generate each other so that the result becomes "une évocation multiple", viz. a whole "série mobile" of metaphors prompted by a given sensation[38]. He defines a poem as a series of metaphors viewed under various angles[39]. The fabric of poetry is vowen by comparisons[40]. The ida of chains of metaphors is a favourite one with many Imagist theorists and poets.

Kahn's own poetry, which is often about love, is mainly stanzaic (he says in the 1897 essay that his efforts are directed towards *le strophe*[41]). It contains rhymes of many, often very sophisticated, kinds. The structural pattern is one line equalling one thought, ie the lines are of different length. His choice of words smacks of conventional poetic diction.

Gourmont was sceptical of *vers libre*. He argued that perfection was found also in poets writing in the old tradition. He intends, he says, to follow the development "during the next twenty years", but, when all is said and done, he is convinced that free verse is a kind of sorcerer's apprentice[42]. He prefers to talk about *vers libéré,* which excludes or includes the mute letters at the poet's discretion.

Free verse is not a *sine qua non* where Hulme and Imagism are concerned. Several Imagists also employed conventional metres, and free verse was used by non-Imagist poets as well. But prosody was a piece in a larger puzzle: not only was it an exemplification of the concept of dynamism, it was also looked upon as an intriguing field of experimentation, and free verse was in tune with the *Zeitgeist* because it is anti-deterministic. English critics did not see it as an audacious provocation, and they emphasized that it is not synonymous with utter laissez-faire within prosody. They insist that free verse has a rhythm of its own, and it is that very rhythm that makes is distinguishable from prose. In England, more than in France, free verse became a predominantly formal device within a fairly limited field, viz. the length and rhythm of verse lines.

Interest in the problem of free verse was reinforced by the upsurge of interest in language. Poets felt that free verse was instrumental in releasing language from its purely deicitic funtion, and linked it to the suggestiveness and evocativeness which, like the Symbolist images, create a feeling of unity of a different order. *Vers libre* was a current topic of discussion in the prefaces to the Imagist anthologies of 1915 and 1916, and in various issues of the periodical *The Egoist*. In an article in that periodical[43], Huntley Carter refers disparagingly to the attempts on the part of the older poets to check the flow of the rhythm. On the contrary, modern poets strive to 'feel' this rhythm (of natural speech, presumably), or to "devise a framework for the eternal flow into which the eternal spirit in human beings is drawn". Carter builds a Bergson-inspired philosophical structure on top of the concept of rhythm: human beings partake of an eternal spirit that is drawn into the continuous flow of existence.

Richard Aldington is considerably more down to earth in another article from the same periodical[44]. He launches a polemical attack on metrical verse, claiming that the complex accented metres were invented by the Provençal poets, who, as a rule, have little to say, and who say badly what little they have to say. What Aldington's postulate boils down to is saying that metrical verse was invented to cover the shallowness of the content so that the form, at least, would shine. Similar thoughts occur in other Imagist critics' works. The old type of verse, Aldington goes on to say, forced the poet to abandon some of his individuality because he was obliged to wedge his material into a previously determined pattern. In free verse, however, the artist sets his own standards, which prevents art from becoming stereotyped. Aldington prefers to talk about "poems in unrhymed cadences". That term was coined by Flint, and it became one of the Imagists' dogmas that cadence should replace metre.

Amy Lowell gives a definition-like description of free verse in her book *Modern American Poetry* (1917): *Vers libre* is "the sense of perfect balance of flow and rhythm". The syllables must "so fall as to continue and increase the movement"; the whole poem must be "as rounded and recurring as the circular swing of a balanced pendulum. It can be fast or slow, it may even jerk, but this perfect swing it must have, even its jerks must follow the central movement"[45]. "The words must be hurried or delayed in reading to fill out the swing"[46], and the cadences are made up of time units "which are in no sense syllabic"[47]. The unit is neither "the foot, the number of syllables, the quantity, or the like. The unit is the strophe, which may be the whole poem, or may only be a part. Each strophe is a complete circle"[48].

Harnessing free verse to his favourite idea that poetry should be read as music, Ezra Pound writes in *The Egoist* that the important thing is that words should not be tumbled together. As could be expected, Pound does not mince matters: *vers libre* has become a pestilence, just as regular verse used to be. The only people who are worse than the 'vers-libristes' are the 'anti-vers-.libristes'. He ends up by brushing the whole dispute aside, saying that things would be far simpler if people knew more about music, and if they would base their discussions on music[49].

According to Marguerite Wilkinson[50], the value of free verse consists in the scope for rhythmical experimentation. And she sums up with some apposite observations: many poets have used the free rhythms beautifully, and many ignoramuses have made a mess of them. The touchstone is the individual poet's worth: those who have acquitted themselves most honourably in the new forms are those who have also excelled in regular rhythms.

Eliot tackles the subject from a slightly different angle in *The Statesman* from 1917[51]: freedom can only exist in cases where there is a background of limitation. Accordingly he states categorically that there is no such thing as free verse in English poetry. But of course it is incumbent on the poet to make clear whether what he writes is intended as poetry or prose.

And that was felt by many of the critics who were concerned with form rather than with content to be the crux of the matter: how to avoid that poetry becomes indistinguishable from prose. Actually, Wilkinson was the only critic who raised the provocative question whether the difference actually matters; is the point not rather whether we enjoy the work? In the article from *The Egoist* quoted above, Aldington is anxious to emphasize that free verse is not identical with prose because it has a shorter and more regular rhythmical constant. That is perhaps meant as an implicit answer to Kahn, who had suggested[52] that free verse could be confused with "une prose poétique, rythmée et nombrée avec une sorte de musique".

Flint sees no difficulty in distinguishing between the two: in prose "the emotions are those that are capable of development in a straight line...In poetry we have a succession of curves. The direction of thought...is wavy and spiral"[53]. Here it seems that content determines form. Fletcher chimes in with the idea of content as an important factor: it is "the rhythm of the line when spoken, which sets poetry apart from prose"[54]. Pope's rhythm was the same in all the lines of his poems. However, that method is artificial as well as unmusical and, if used today, "it gives the effect of monotonous rag-time", and it does not allow full scope "for emotional development"[55]. Poetry is capable of "as many gradations in cadence as music is in time". We can "gradually increase or decrease our tempo, creating accelerando and rallentando effects...The good poem is that in which all these effects are used to convey the underlying emotions of its author"[56].

In an essay from 1908, Hulme wrote that metrical verse is appropriate for the greater individual expressiveness and spontaneity[57]. However, modern poetry is small-scale and intimate, "a tentative and half-shy manner of looking at things". Putting it into the straitjacket of a regular metre would be like "putting a child into armour"[58]. Hulme's own poems are 'half-shy' in the sense that 'greater' subjects like patriotism, idealism, and morality are left out of consideration. Love comes literally in through the back door, either in the shape of suggestive eroticism, or as a slightly ironical abstraction. To Hulme, free verse meant an unequal number of syllables in the lines. The line is a unit of thought and/or imagery. His poems only very occasionally make use of rhymes, and, since they are so short, the problem of stanzaic division is only of marginal interest.

Dance

Dance – the art of dancing and the performance of the dancer – naturally captivated the interests of the post-Positivist artists. It was dynamism visualized. Dance is able to throw a clear light on what the artist's task is, and what perfection in art means. Already Gourmont had stressed the visual element in poetry, and in *Chemin de Velours* (1902) he said that the aesthetic feelings are those that reverberate through the whole body[59].

Another source of inspiration was the Japanese Noh, to which several references are made by poets and critics in the first two decades of the 20th century. The code word for Noh is energy. The concentration of arranged movements of the body produces control of body and mind. The task of the body is to express all the feelings that the roles contain; masks and costumes contribute to a description of the character. Female parts were played by men wearing masks. The mask is, as Lester puts it[60], a technique to convey an inner experience through objectivization. It is not difficult to see here a forestalling of what Eliot was to call the objective correlative.

Dance was the visual embodiment of an art form and was therefore eagerly studied by an age that was fond of painting and sculpture, and which saw the sisterhood of the arts as an aesthetic given. One of Gaudier-Brzeska's best-known sculptures is called *The Dancer*.

Hulme, who was always concerned with what Pound called "the point of maximum energy", was deeply fascinated by dance and dancers. Dance, he says, is among the phenomena that give us sudden uplifts[61]. It retains an idea at the same time as it dwells upon a point [62]. 'Sudden uplifts' and 'dwelling upon a point' would be an appropriate characterization of the technique that he used and the effect he strove to obtain in his poems. Hulme also saw a relationship between the rhythm of music and the rhythm of the body. Using a synaesthetic image he says that listening to music is like the rhythmical movement of a ship[63], and he discerns a likeness between the poet's expression and the dancer's performance of his art.

Though he was a big hulk of a man. Hulme would have liked to become a dancer, and throughout his life he was attracted to the art of ballet. Images of dance and dancers frequently occur in his criticial oeuvre. What appealed to him were the control of the body and the elegance of movement that are characteristic of competent dancers. He sees the female dancer as the embodiment of beauty, but he adds that even the most independent dancer has to have her face powdered and wear high heels[64], implicitly acknowledging that even ideals cannot exist in an unadulterated state. In a letter to Edward Marsh, Hulme talks about the possibility of transferring names of states of mind to physical objects in art, and he finds it important that we are able to "live our feelings into" outward shapes[65].

On several occasions he refers to a red dancer, who is interesting for her 'effects', of course, but, more importantly, for her intimations of intensity of meaning. She is "cindery", ie potentially able to rise above the humdrum everyday existence, she is "more than herself", viz. an objectified state of mind in the beholder plus a living manifestation of her art. What she achieves comes close to the Kantian *Ding an sich*, which has "evolved painfully from the clay" (which is what 'cindery' means in Hulme's idiosyncratic terminology) and exists out of time[66]. The beholder will be able to see some of his perceptions projected onto, and personified in, the red-dressed dancing woman. Thus the beholder can literally see the artist's intention.

But the point is *also* that dancing is an art where the performance of the individual dancer is hard to distinguish from the art of dancing itself. Dancing is an art form rendered visible. We may refer to the concluding lines of Yeats' poem *Among School Children:* "How can we know the dancer from the dance?". The performer, ie the concrete manifestation, is inseparable from the art, ie the abstract concept. Dance, capitalized, is seen in and embodied by, the dancer – and unthinkable without his or her performance. That interaction between the abstract, or the general, and the concrete, or the specific, is a permanent challenge to Hulme and the Imagists.

CHAPTER EIGHT

HULME'S PHILOSOPHY

INTRODUCTION

Hulme was, in all areas, a self-taught person: he was not a professional philosopher or art historian, nor did he hold a university degree in literature, His theories are fragmentary and derivative, mostly published in some articles in the periodical *New Age* from December 1915 to February 1916.

In his thinking, philosophy, religion, politics, and aesthetics are closely interwoven. Consequently, a treatment of his philosophical ideas must necessarily take into consideration several different branches of his intellectual activity as well. He also wrote a few poems, and although they amount to less than 300 lines altogether, they are clear indications of what he thought poetry should be. His theoretical writings are rambling, sometimes repetitive, even contradictory. Conventional terms and concepts are often given a slight twist (eg fancy and imagination), and they alternate with novel ideas and formulations eg about the relationship between language and reality ("We live in a room. Did we make it, or did we just decorate it?" he asks). He regularly indulges in name-dropping, and what he has adopted from other thinkers (eg Bergson) is mostly indirectly conveyed, but usually clearly perceptible – and sometimes half-digested.

It is impossible to establish a coherent theoretical or critical system on the basis of his reflections and *obiter dicta*. But then again, he did not strive to, or have the time to, construct a complete and unassailable philosophical or critical edifice. Hulme's philosophy and art criticism rest on a firm moral basis: to him, aesthethics is unimaginable without a moral, even religious, dimension. Yet his poetry does not preach a moral. That point is worth emphasizing, for he wrote during a period, viz. the yerars immediately before and during the Great War, when a good deal of the poetry that was written was edifying and patrriotic (eg Rupert Brooke).

Hulme's ideas remained unchanged from their inception and onwards. Thus the idea of moral and social development remained one of his pet aversions, and his belief in Original Sin was never shaken. Both his *Speculations*, edited by Middleton Murray, and *Further Speculations*, edited by Sam Hynes, are admittedly unsystematic and associational, a half-finished house. Still, both of them do contain acute observations, and it is possible to form some idea of he was getting at.

It is characteristic of his thinking that he rarely reaches any kind of conclusion. Man is organized chaos, he says[1], and liable to revert to chaos any moment. However, he does not tell us anything about the nature of that chaos, or who or what prevents or hastens the fall into the abyss. He foresees a new departure within art and is satisfied that it will be neither Futurism, post-Impressionism, nor Cubism. But he leaves his readers in the dark with regard to the exact character of the new type of art[2]. It is only fair to add, though, that, most often, he recognizes the insufficiency of his suggestions, and that a generally deprecating attitude is typical of his presentation. One point where he does not mince matters, however, is his criticism of the Renaissance. During that period, the task of art was held to convey 'truth to nature', and from there it was but a short step to look upon 'imitation of the real' as art, which Hulme calls "a fallacious inference".

His prose writings are interesting not only because they are typical of Imagist theorizing. Many of the motifs we find in his poems occur in his prose reflections as well, and he gives illuminating and relevant parallels from the other arts.

Argumentation

In his treatment of philosophical and critical issues, Hulme's parts are superior to his wholes. His beginnings are often profound and very promising, but they tend to peter out. He never doubted that he was right: his statements are presented axiomatically with an air of 'it is the case that…' about them.

In-depth analyses are few and far between. He likes to clinch an issue with one or two epigrammatic flourishes, which he repeats in slightly different formulations. And when he proceeds to argue, the result is often muddled, or even dubious. His definitions, such as they are, too often read like rash assertions, and he likes to put his message across as if it was the outcome of his own intellectual efforts. He is not prone to acknowledge his indebtedness to either predecessors or contemporaries, and he shows no little intransigence with opinions that differ from his own. Even in cases where he deals with other theorists with whose ideas he feels in sympathy, he tends to swerve off from the person's views and drift over to his own hobbyhorses. A case in point is his treatment of Bergson, which is eminently 'Bergson as I see him'.

When Hulme juxtaposes or compares two ideas, he does not attempt to show that either of them is logically untenable or linguistically meaningless.

Nor does he break them down into their constituent parts to demonstrate eg that the latter are mutually incompatible. He does not analyse the relation between the two, and he does not prove anything in the proper sense of the word. What he does do is to replace some axioms with others, substituting one set of value judgements for another. That is a far cry from a genuine linguistic or logical analysis. Hulme discusses abstracts by stating what in his opinion they ought to mean. His comments are frequently shrewd, and the angles from which he views conventional ideas are often baffling in their originality. However, his argumentation has little cogency, not always reaching logical or easy-to-follow levels. His final verdicts are intuitive.

Absolutes

Hulme's anti-Positivist stance is apparent in his attitude to what he calls Absolutes. He does not explain, let alone analyse, what an Absolute is; nor does he account for what confers the dignity of an Absolute on a concept or an idea. On the other hand, he does not doubt that Absolutes exist, and they determine the content and direction of his thinking. Only very few concepts qualify for inclusion, and foremost among them are God and Original Sin; those two are the bedrock of his philosophy and criticism. It would be entirely misleading to call his prose works religious disquisitions: explicit references to eg the Bible are few and far between, but the fulcrum of his reflections is indubitably Christian.

Hulme acknowledges space and time as objective categories, but he hastens to add that the religious attitude should be the guideline of all thinking, and it has the same objective validity as space and time[3]. Characteristically, Hulme gives no arguments to underpin that assertion, but space and time are definitely inferior as Absolutes to Original Sin, which defines man's position in the world: man is irrevocably imperfect, and his only hope is divine intervention.

That is the reason why Hulme considered the idea of social progress an absurdity, and that explains why he preferred the art forms that he called geometrical because he saw a parallel between them and the religious quest for austerity and permanence [4]. Original Sin makes man a circumscribed being; accordingly, Utopianism is not only futile, it is sinful. What appealed to him in the idea of Original Sin was the implied necessity of discipline – man is, and should know that he is, a limited being. The doctrine of redemption did not interest him[5]. He even went so far as to maintain that belief or non-belief in the Fall of Man is at the root of all genuine social and political thought. Ultimately, Socialism and Liberalism are all of a piece[6]. On the other hand he was not blind to the dilemma he was saddled with, viz. to what extent freedom of thought and action, which he also advocated, are compatible with a belief in Original Sin[7]. He never approached a solution to that problem.

What he objects to in the Renaissance was that it was the period when a religious schism occurred, and when the anthropomorphization of art began. That 'human-making', which has continued ever since in the arts, led to a concern with standards that were satisfactory to man[8], and that humanistically inspired satisfaction has erroneously been taken to be the only possible type of satisfaction[9]. In the Renaissance, a new world view (Hulme uses the German word *Weltanschauung*) emerges, and it caused people to forget the tragic meaning of life, which is what really matters to Hulme: a critique of satisfaction would have to be based on religion, thus revealing our unconscious, human-based, hence worthless, canons[10].

Renaissance art was dependent on "pleasure in the reproduction of human and natural forms"[11], a 'smoothness' that Hulme with his predilection for what was 'hard and dry' was bound to detest. Unfortunately, Renaissance art has come to be taken as being equivalent to Art capitalized. But once again, Hulme has to back-pedal: Pascal, who was, incidentally, a deeply religious man, is an exception to post-Renaissance decline.

HULME AND SCIENCE

Hulme attacks the type of person he calls 'the naturalist' for having subjected himself to a kind of metaphysics, viz. the illusion that science provides the only possible type of factual knowledge[12]. The implication is that Original Sin belongs in the category of factual knowledge. Hulme repeatedly taunts Positivist science for its pretentions to being able to give us truth. Science and religion were to him poles apart: the knowledge that science is able to furnish is seemingly complete, yet insufficient when juxtaposed to the divinely inspired, hence perfect, knowledge provided by religion.

It is in line with his hostility to science that Hulme was also violently opposed to determininsm. He rejected the scientists' optimistic contention that, given more precise methods, it would be possible to detect still more 'natural laws', and that the existing 'laws' would become increasingly reliable. To Hulme, the universe was essentially unpredictable – if not, how could one account for the existence of the Free Will, which is another of Hulme's Absolutes?

Paradoxically, in his poetry, Hulme consistently uses the preferred procedure of Positivist science, viz. observation and conclusion. His poems are neither introspective nor reflective, but emphatically visual: an observer, who is often 'outside' the poem, sees things and presents the results of that observation.

Hulme's attack on the scientists' reliance on their methods as the only path to true knowledge bears resemblance to Derrida's reflections on what he calls the 'logocentrism' of Western civilization as the paradigm that makes thinking at all possible. In Hulme's opinion, science should know its place. The pronouncements of the individual sciences are appropriate for specific and limited purposes, but they have only a relative validity. Science cannot yield universal truth[13].

Bergson

At first sight, it may seem surprising that Hulme should be so influenced by Bergson, who was anything but an absolutist. It was the Frenchman's mode of presentation that appealed to a devotee of images like Hulme: what Bergson did was to use introspection and employ some metaphors that gave a vivid and plastic idea of what he discovered to be his mental life[14]. Sometimes Hulme takes over the French philosopher's terminology lock, stock, and barrel; sometimes he develops his own theories and categories, which, however, show unmistakable similarities to Bergson's system.

Dichotomies

Hulme's thinking proceeds in terms of dichotomies. Two of the contrasts that are basic to his philosophy are movement (or flux) versus stasis (or poise). Like Bergson, Hulme saw reality as a flux of interpenetrating elements[15]. That, however, does not render impossible the existence of permanent concepts like intuition and intellect. Equally, Hulme is certain that in some respects man is not subjected to movement: evolution is not operative within morals, and Hulme sees this very constancy as a prerequisite and a guarantee of change[16]. That may sound paradoxical, but what it boils down to is that Hulme denies the principle of the inevitability of general progress, but not the possibility of desirable changes within specific areas. Thus he is in no doubt that valuable new departures have taken place within the literature of his day.

Intuition versus Intellect

In his treatment of intuition, Hulme leans heavily on Bergson. Indeed, in the chapter called *Bergson's Theory of Art*, which forms part of the *Speculations*, it is hard to tell when Hulme is quoting the Frenchman, and when he is speaking in his own voice[17]. Following Bergson, Hulme sees human consciousness as a blend of two complementary and interdependent components, viz. *intuition* and *intellect*. The two perform a division of labour in that we have an intuition of our mental life, and we know the mechanical world by intellect[18].

Intuition is a very potent force to Hulme: it is at the root of all philosophy. However, its real nature is shrouded in obscurity, and instead of defining it, Hulme furnishes some illustrative examples of how it works: intuition gives us a clear perception of the totality of a face without our being able to define the individual parts that make it up. Intuition is like being on a river and sensing its interpenetrating tendencies[19], William James would have nodded approval.

The point for Hulme is that "the flux of interpenetrated elements" that add up to make reality is "unseizable by the intellect"[20]. Accordingly, we can only be granted a complete understanding of, and insight into, reality by the use of intuition, and not by the "usual mechanical processes"[21]. Intuition enables a person to get to the heart of a subject – a kind of insight denied to the intellect[22]. Hulme goes a step further: the distinguishing feature of creative artists is that they are endowed with intuition, and art is a rendering of the reality underlying the "interpenetrated elements"[23]. According to Hulme, intuition can cope with issues where the intellect will have to resign. But he does not say whether intuition is a stage that can be reached by non-artists, eg by the beholder of a picture or a reader of poetry – or perhaps by any other privileged person.

Manifolds

Another important bipartite division in Hulme's philosophy – not borrowed from Bergson, but clearly derivable from the intuition/intellect dichotomy – is the distinction between *extensive* and *intensive manifolds*. An extensive manifold is a mechanistic thing, a complex entity that can be broken down into separate compartments, and the separation is performred by the intellect[24]. Hulme's example of an extensive manifold is the world around us. However, there are some complex phenomena that cannot be decomposed into discrete entities, they are interpenetrated "at deep level" (a Bergsonian term)[25] in such a way that the intellect cannot grasp them. That qualitative multiplicity is called an intensive manifold, "a condition whole…whose parts cannot be even conceived as existing separately"[26], and it can only be comprehended by intuition.

Hulme illustrates his point by referring to the Free Will, which is incomprehensible in mechanistic terms – but which demonstrably exists. The inference is that there is more to reality than the intellect can account for. Other candidates for inclusion into the category of intensive manifolds are the two Bergson-inspired hypotheses of *élan* and *évolution*[27]: it is as impossible to dissect evolution as it is to anticipate its direction; as a matter of fact we do not know what is actually going on in the process of evolution. Bergson had taken up a demonstratively anti-teleological and anti-Darwinian attitude in his theory of evolution – even if he used the same biological terms as Darwin. To Bergson, evolution is "a separation out of elements which interpenetrated in the original impulse"[28]. Hulme interprets that to mean that the process of evolution is "the insertion of more and more freedom into matter". That insertion is anti-mechanistic and anti-teleological.

On this point as on several others in his philosophical system, Bergson's presentation is diffuse and inconclusive, but Hulme's 'adaptation' does not make things easier for his readers. Thus one might ask why everything does not end up in chaos if the 'insertion' is totally arbitrary. And it is surely remarkable that, in order to put his message across, Hulme has to resort to deterministic formulations: 'direction', 'destined', 'resulting'.

Humanism and Religion

Much of late 19th century thinking, oriented as it was towards man and society., was repellent to Hulme, who considered it trivial and irrelevant. Hence it is paradoxical that his poetry should be essentially non-religious and centre on man's position in this world. Even non-naturalistic concepts like eg sunsets are placed by Hulme in decidedly everyday and recognizable contexts.

In his conception of human nature, Hulme contrasts the religious view and the humanistic view. As he sees it, the 'religious attitude' cannot find expression in terms of the categories of our life because those categories are relative. As a consequence of Original Sin, man and his life on earth are stigmatised with imperfection, whereas religion rests on the idea of perfection[29]. What Hulme objects to in humanism is that is poses human life and human standards as the ultimate measure of all values. Hulme spurns the idea that man is fundamentally good, and the 'canons of satisfaction' are false because they fail to recognize the tragedy of life. Post-Renaissance art and philosophy have been vitiated by focusing on man, and even if Hulme approves of the element of freedom implicit in humanism, he attacks it because it represents the highest manifestation of the contemptible "vital"[30]. Hulme uses 'vital' in its etymological sense, viz. 'what is concerned with life' (*vita*).

Hulme recognized the existence of a 'higher world', and he was confident that some people could have epiphanic moments that would yield insight into that world. Characteristically, he is very reticent about the nature of that 'higher world' and about the kind of people who are granted such visions. He breaks off half-way, stressing that such ecstasies cannot be induced artificially, eg by drinking or drug-taking – even though he is prepared to admit that some people have produced original thoughts in their drunkenness[31]. The interesting thing is that, in his poems, Hulme strove to produce similar epiphanies in his readers. However, the insights were not of a 'higher world', but of this world.

Hulme's basic grievance against humanism was its scepticism where religion was concerned. So he envisaged a new age that would be comparable to the Middle Ages in "the subordination of man to certain values"[32]. He obviously had religious values in mind. However, he leaves the influence of the Roman-Catholic church in post-Renaissance Europe entirely out of consideration, and the idea of a 'new age' is hard to reconcile with Hulme's repeated strictures on concepts like evolution, development, and progress. The idea of progress is, in his opinion, nothing but "substitute religion"[33].

Perhaps Hulme thought that the really valid categories would be reborn on a different level than merely sublunary ones. Another remarkable fact is that in his prose writings he flatly rejects the idea of infinity, and yet his poems abound with thinly veiled allusions to that very idea: stars, sky, ships, things being removed to an unknown somewhere. But his scenes are town scenes – he clearly prefers the 'limited' town to the open countryside. Perhaps he had had enough when, as a young man, he worked in the open spaces of Canada.

Values

In spite of his somewhat rigid categorizations, Hulme denies the possibility of a hierarchy of values. He also maintains that there are no ultimate principles on which knowledge can be based: we must be satisfied with an endless succession of analogies that give us a feeling of controlling chaos. The images of his poems are a vehicle for reducing chaos.

Hulme does not offer any definition or in-depth treatment of the lower-ranging Absolutes to which he refuses to give undisputed validity even if he acknowledges their existence. He admits that "pure seeing of the whole process is impossible"[34], for which reason any philosophy is reduced to the status of "valet to the Absolute". Yet he did not go to the same lengths as the Deconstructionists, who ask what the ontological status of 'ultimate truths' actually is.

According to Sir Herbert Read, Hulme had planned, but never managed to finish, a work that was intended to deliver a decisive blow to the idea that the world is one, and that everything is describable by means of words. We also have Hulme's outline for a book on Modern Theories of Art, with the headlines and the content of some of the chapters. In that book, Bergson was to take pride of place, and Croce and Lipps ("the greatest writer on aesthetics") were to be honourable runners-up.

Conclusion

Hulme's philosophical thinking is difficult to follow. His language is metaphoric, which gives the impression that many of his assumptions are seen at one remove, so to speak. Taken as a whole, his philosophical output is paradoxical: intuition is held by him to be the root of all philosophy; yet Original Sin is an Absolute from which all thinking starts. He believes in the Bergsonian *élan*, yet he is a determined opponent of progress. Indeed he was so much of what we would today call a reactionary that some critics have labelled him a crypto-Fascist (he spoke favourably of Sorel). He says, not without some justification, that it was never made clear what progress was supposed to lead to[35], and yet he often refers to 'evolution'. He attacks the idea of continuity[36], and permanent stasis was anathema to him. Still, he bases a good deal of his philosophy on the contrast between flux and poise – indeed, his poems are intended to furnish momentary stops in the current of his readers' thoughts. On the one hand, he maintains that dynamism is a given thing, on the other he wants the forward drive to be temporarily stopped by his striking images.

Hulme is aware of the social misery surrounding him, yet he rejects the idea of social development. In one passage he claims that movement came into the world immediately after creation, in another he raises the question how much was created before man made his appearance in the world[37].

Add to this, there is a good deal of hair-splitting and confusion in his terminology. He takes exception to explanations of life in mechanistic terms, and he is generally suspicious of what he calls mechanistic thinking [38]. Instead, he favours instinctive or 'vital' thinking, as he calls it, thus making 'vital' an asset, whereas in his theory of art it is a decided liability. He admits that there is some interaction between ideals and material conditions[39] (he does not seem to have studied Marx in any detail). But he is ambiguous as to which of the two takes precedence. In one passage he claims that ideas may be the cause of material conditions[40], in another he insists that ideas are determined by material conditions[41]. He is convinced that human nature is fixed, yet he believes in the freedom of the will[42].

Hulme looks upon man as chaos organized[43], and he draws a parallel between the human organism and the structure of the world. But he denies the possibility of an all-embracing logical position[44]. The soul is spirit, but personality is held to depend on the body[45]. One of his many potentially fertile observations that a reader would like to have seen elaborated, but which is left hanging in the air, is a rather off-hand remark about ideals versus ideas. He does not mind ideals; what he objects to are the stupid ideas that are often advanced to defend them. Thus, the ideals of liberal democracy are good as far as they go, but highly objectionable ideas have been expressed to support those ideals. A reader would be thankful to be told how it is possible to discuss ideals if ideas are left out of account.

CHAPTER NINE

HULME'S AESTHETICS

INTRODUCTION

Pound said that Hulme's writings had little relevance for, and connection with, what happened within aesthtics in the years 1910-1912[1]. Not all modern readers would subscribe to that categorical statement. His critical grounding may be insufficient, and his assumptions – also in this field – idiosyncratic. But he was indubitably in line with, sometimes even in the forefront of, theoretical speculation from approximately 1908 until his death in 1917. Indeed, he was not only a catalyst for much of the aesthetic thinking of the Edwardian and early Georgian ages, he also focused attention on quite a few of the issues that have been significant in the aesthetic debate down through the centuries, seeing them in the light of his own opinions and of the aesthetic climate of his age.

Hulme endeavoured to get to grips with some basic aesthetic problems, and within the field of aesthetic criticism and theory he used his investigative powers and his considerable shrewdness of observation at least as energetically as most contemporary critics and poets used theirs. He was no ignoramus where music, painting and sculpture were concerned, and he had planned to write a book dealing with the history of art from Plato to Bergson because he found that, in existing books on art, aesthetics had not been paid sufficient attention[2]. The project never materialized.

Hulme was perfectly aware that what he was presenting was loosely sketched thoughts rather than thoroughgoing theoretical argumentation and system building. As a critic, he is often original, dogmatic rather than precise, intuitive rather than argumentative – but never boring or really malicious. He has no theoretical ideal or ideals whom he strives to imitate or emulate, as eg the Neo-Classics worshipped Homer or Horace. On the whole, it is remarkable how little he draws on forerunners or contemporaries, and that may account, in part, for the desultoriness of his criticism. He does a good deal of free-hand drawing, and his presentation is selective and idiosyncratic. His vague use of concepts like 'image', 'analogy', 'nature', and several others is frustrating, and his haziness when dealing with eg 'idea', 'form' and 'content' may cause many a reader to tear his hair.

Hulme often surprises his readers: he is anything but a Romanticist, yet, like Coleridge, he is intrigued by the distinction between fancy and imagination (which latter he characterizes as an intensive manifold). However, he hardly ever mentions Coleridge's name, and his reflections on fancy and imagination are at odds with those of the author of *Biographa Literaria*. He is opposed to late Victorian poetic practice, yet his references to Tennyson are not unequivocally negative, and he pays tribute to Swinburne for the musicality of his verse.

The Purpose of Art

The purpose of art is to satisfy a desire and to make people like the merely healthy[3]. Of course quite a lot hinges on the definition of words like 'desire' and 'healthy'. Hulme is a bit ambiguous on this point. He was averse to the idea that art – including literature – should have a message. Yet, on the other hand he says that the philosophy of art is meant to demonstrate the non-perfectibility of man[4]: the poet dwells on a point, and that concentration gives delight to the poet and a kind of uplift to the reader. And the artist need not feel guilty because he educates 'ordinary' people[5], for his task is "to penetrate the veil" that has been placed between ourselves and reality[6]. However, poetry is *also* amusement and relaxation[7]; it does not always aspire to infinite nobleness, and, as Hulme drily adds, few people would understand that anyway[8].

The object of art is not representation. Hulme often pays tribute to artists who sacrifice representation, eg Cubist painters. What matters is rendering the *vision* in such a way that the artist is satisfied and the recipient won over. In Hulme's phrasing, many people can build a dome, but it takes an artist to render the mood of it[9].

Hulme is a little wavering on the complex issue of art versus nature. Mimesis is brushed aside: art is not to reproduce or interpret nature, yet contact with nature is indispensable in order to extract facts that have so far been ignored[10]. But then again, although art is not mimetic, Hulme seems to think that artists are somehow guilty when they change nature radically[11]. The conclusion would seem to be that the objects of *natura naturata* should not be rendered with photographic exactitude, but 'heightened', as the critics of the 18th century called it, eg by being viewed in a revealing flash or from an unexpected angle. Hulme instances an everyday thing like a railway line, which is primarily known for its usefulness. However, if seen from above, ie in an unconventional perspective, the line becomes beautiful[12]. So, what confers beauty on objects is not their outward appearance or functionalism *per se* (his italics), but the new way of looking at them[13]. Our consciousness is a sea in a state of permanent movement; the artist makes "a fixed model of one of these transient waves and enables you to isolate it out and to perceive it in yourself"[14].

Dichotomies

Hulme's theory of art, like his philosophy, is to a large extent based on dichotomies. As we saw in an earlier chapter, he opposes intensive and extensive manifolds, and intuition and intellect. Such pairs seem to make up the sum total within a given area of knowledge. They may be contrary or supplementary approaches to an artistic problem, and, as Hulme sees it, *tertium non datur*. Hulme cannot be called a middle-of-the-road man. If, on a rare occasion, he has to admit that the subject is not exhausted by his usual procedure, alternative options are looked askance at, or reluctantly let in through the back door. It goes without saying that Hulme's tactic means that a good many corners are cut.

Form

Since art was to Hulme synonymous with a passionate desire for accuracy, it is no wonder that he was intensely preoccupied with form. His poems are form made visible.

Hulme distinguishes between two types of form that may be conveniently called form and Form (he never uses capital letters himself about this problem). The two 'forms' illustrate his abstract/concrete dichotomy. The individual work of art represents a fusion of form and content, but 'behind', and independently of, any work of art, there is an abstraction, viz. Form *per se*. Hulme advises a budding artist to begin with a well-known Form and then, gradually, assert his independence[15], ie find his own form. But he emphasizes that, in a given work of art, it is not possible to consider form in isolation (many modern critics would agree on this point), and he says explicitly that form cannot provide an aesthetic experience[16]. And yet he views Form as a rational, indeed almost moral, factor in that it contributes to setting boundaries for content: Hulme had an almost Puritanical obsession with limitation.

Geometric versus Vital Art

In terms of form, the great distinction to Hulme is between geometric and vital art: each of the two corresponds to "a certain general attitude towards the world"[17].

Pre-Renaissance art was, like Egyptian and Oriental art, largely two-dimensional, which may be the reason why Hulme chose to call it geometric. Besides it was based on hard, uncompromising shapes. What also spoke in its favour was that, unlike Renaissance and post-Renaissance art, it was not individualized, a fact that appealed immensely to the anti-humanist Hulme. Geometric art is inorganic, hence more permanent[18]. It designs the human body in a way that is separated from the world, thus demonstrating the divide between man and nature. Picasso's paintings, for instance, are "studies of a special kind of machinery"[19]. The pyramids are other examples of geometric art: they are "a refuge from the flux and impermanence of outside nature"[20], ie another exemplification of stasis versus flux.

The second decade of the 20th century witnessed a growing fascination with Indian and Byzantine art. Cubism seemed to be a contemporary exemplification of geometric art, and non-figurative sculptors like Epstein and Gaudier-Brzeska were respected members of the coterie of artists in which Hulme was a rather prominent figure. Hulme claimed to have learnt the appreciation of geometric art from his friend Epstein. An important reason why his enthusiasm was aroused was that he saw, in the mosaics at Ravenna and Byzantium, the expression of a religious attitude to life.

Geometric art never strives to meet the current need of merely hedonistic satisfaction, or to live up to prevalent criteria of beauty. Vital art is, as the name indicates, centred on the attraction of human life on earth, and the human body. It is concerned with conventional conceptions of natural beauty, which means that it caters for man's transitory inclinations[21]. But 'pure form' is antivital, hence a reflection of the divine. However, by reducing the forms of nature to 'hard' geometric lines, an artist could hope to make manifest an idea of limitation and imperfection.

Hulme was convinced that a people's art runs parallel with its philosophy and world view. Vital art arises in situations when people feel sure of themselves and their position in the world. And he postulated a connection between primitive culture and the highest and purest art form[22]. "The simple and its development was bound to offer the greatest possibility of happiness to the man disquited by the obscurity and entanglement of phenomena", as Alun Jones puts it[23].

Paradoxically Hulme, who hated the idea of cultural development, had a biological view of art: an artistic convention flourishes, grows old, and falls into decline[24]: the masters of Renaissance painting refined a theory that was in embryo when they started, but which has 'by now' outlived itself[25]. Hulme hoped to see a revival of geometric art, which had been submerged by the humanist cult of the Renaissance, and he would like to see art becoming the precursor of the emergence of a similar attitude to the world[26]. It will be seen that Hulme's aspirarions are reminiscent of Shelley's hopes for the artist to become the legislator of mankind (which means that, for all Hulme's deprecatory remarks, art to him *was* didactic). It may be added that Hulme considered Shelley's poetry shallow because it lacked a religious ingredient.

What Hulme objected to in vital art was its superficiality because it cultivated a sense of beauty that people imagine they have, but which is not a real need. Hulme is not very explicit either about the nature of such needs, or whether the needs of the artist and the public coincide. Nor does he give any suggestion to explain why needs change, or how he could be sure that he knew the 'real needs'. He felt that there was more sincerity in the art of Cézanne, to whom the multifarious forms of nature are reducible to three, viz. *cône, cylindre et sphére*[27].

Classical versus Romantic

Another important distinction made by Hulme is that between Classical and Romantic, to which he devotes a long essay in his *Speculations*. That distinction, too, ultimately rests on a religious foundation, and, as is usual with Hulme, it is more than a theory of art, it is the formulation of an attitude to life.

The issue is discussed by Taine – without the religious overtones: Classicism and Romanticism are prolongations of two phases of knowledge, two ways of placing oneself vis-à-vis reality, and of apprehending it[28]. Hulme widens the perspective: the two concepts differ in their view of man, and to Hulme the human and the divine must be clearly separated[29], Classicism representing limitation and Romanticism the infinite possibilities[30]. As Hulme sees it, Classicism demonstrates the permanence of human nature and also the belief in the Deity[31]. To Romanticism, man is inherently good, but that perspective was irreconcilable with Hulme's belief in Original Sin.

Hulme calls Romanticism "spilt religion"[32], probably the most scathing criticism he could think of. He attacks it for its aspirations to perfection[33], for, as everybody knows, man never reaches a state of perfection. That is the reaon why Romantic poetry is so "gloomy" and Romantic art in general so "slack". It cultivates the metaphor of frustrated flight[34] (Hulme would seem to have a valid point there), whereas Classical poetry (which is neither exemplified nor defined) is characterized by reservation and holding back.

To Hulme, post-Renaissance art and philosophy are essentially Romantic. That seems to to be an unduly sweeping generalization: what about Neo-Classicism and the Age of Enlightenment? But also, Hulme's conception of Romantic poetry is peculiar: among poets he mentions Byron and Lamartine, but not Wordsworth, Coleridge or Keats, and his attacks on the Romantic poets is lacking in focus.

Beauty

Hulme agrees with Plato that "the object of aesthetic contemplation is something framed apart by itself – simply being itself as end and not as means"[35], and he echoes Kant when he states that we ought to remove the feeling of guilt vis-à-vis what is 'useless'.

As is the case with form, beauty, too, is bipartite in Hulme's perception. Beauty capitalized is an abstract concept of which the individual beautiful objects are illustrations[36]. Beauty confers an aura of eternity on the individual work of art. Hulme's point is that art creates Beauty, but "a lexicon of beauty" is "elastic", as he puts it[37]. However, not all objects are, or can be made, beautiful: miners are a case in point, and though Hulme's ideas of beauty are mainly associated with town life, he has some reservations where cars are concerned. For the creation of beauty, a selection is necessary; such selection might eg consist in the choice of an unusual angle so as to make the beholder see things in a new way. Thus, a train in itself is nothing out of the ordinary, but if it is hidden in vapour, it has a beauty potential. Had he seen Monet's picture?

In Hulme's opinion, beauty (like reality) never appears in a continuum, but in discrete moments of attention as the reward of a conscious effort (stasis versus flux again). That statement is an implicit confirmation of his definition of literature as "a method of sudden arrangements of commonplaces"[38], but it is also an appropriate description of his own practice: 'sudden' on account of the quick impact of the pictures, 'commonplaces' with reference to the down-to-earth subjects of his poems. The gist of his criticism of Yeats is that the latter seeks refuge in a supernatural world that can only be conjured up by means of symbols. Hulme emphatically pulls things down to earth: even in the toilet and its truth it is possible to experience a momentary poetic feeling![39]

A certain amount of »detachment" is required in the reader as well as in the poet, but beauty is not the prerogative of an elite: the reader who experiences beauty may very well wear a workman's clothes[40]. On the other hand, Hulme is not blind to the artist's difficulties when dealing with beauty: he is up against current standards of taste. Ordinary people have stereotyped and uniform ideals of beauty, and they are bound to collide with the artist's beauty, which is "necessarily consciously made"[41]. Hulme's canon was not photographic likeness, but a scene or a situation *vu à travers un tempérament*.

Art determines man's idea of beauty: the man in the street will find a wood scene inherently captivating because he has seen so many pictures showing sylvan scenes[42]. But, as Hulme points out, since people's tastes are demonstrably coloured by what they meet in the arts, the educational responsibility and duty of the artist becomes so much greater. Hulme is dimly aware of the enormity of the task, and once more we see how didacticism creeps into his aesthetic reflections.

In accordance with his scepticism about non-religious Absolutes, Hulme repeatedly warns against identifying Beauty with 'the ideal'. The ideal can very well be morally tainted – Hulme instances love and hate[43]. Hence such themes must be treated artistically so as not to lead to "easy understanding". In the beauty of art, as in life, there are gaps between light and shade; in fact both are reminiscent of a chessboard where pieces are moved around.

Creation

When talking about artistic creation, Hulme naturally exemplifies with the art he knows best, viz. poetry. The starting-point of the composition of a work or art is a sense datum; it may be fleeting and liable to disappear at short notice, but it gives the impressionable observer an awareness of the artistic potential of the datum. Hulme illustrates his point with a girl leaning out of a window one morning: that observation prompts "a vague something" in a beholder, something that is "expressible", but which is not enough in itself.

The basis of all art is an observation that prompts a mood in the artist. The next step is for the observation to be cast into the mould called art. Any creator must submit to some rules if he is to produce art. The datum is the content, and the demands of the medium in which the artist works are the form.

Artistic creation was to Hulme an intensive manifold, for it is not a synthesis of elements. He had a theory of what we would today call paradigms of perception. Also in this area he is intrigued by the relationship between the general and the specific. Perception runs in certain moulds, he says. In ordinary perception we never see things with their individual characteristics, but only types[44]. The artist disentangles the classification, penetrating the veil between ourselves and reality[45]. Hulme quotes with approval Bergson's definition of artistic creation as "a process of discovery and disentanglement"[46].

Hulme's implicit point is that for such revelation to be successful, eg within literature, images and analogies are indispensable. The artist does not create new worlds: literature is the creation of a *different* world (his italics), the construction of states of reference where the reader "thinks himself into an artificial situation"[47]. Thus the artist becomes an intermediary between reality and the beholder, and he becomes what he is in the etymological sense of the word, viz. a maker – of images revealing glimpses of insight into the actually existing world.

HULME AND POLITICS

Religion is the umbrella concept for all Hulme's thinking, and his aesthetic theories find a parallel in his view of politics and of mankind in general. Also his fondness for clear-cut categorization is apparent within the area of politics.

The classical (in the Hulmean sense, ie the opposite of romantic) view of man is pessimistsic. The only way for man to achieve something valuable is to submit to discipline[48], and the touchstone of discipline is Original Sin. In a sweeping generalization Hulme asserts that the great dividing line within social and political thought is between those who believe in the Fall of Man, and those who do not believe in it. And he points out, with no little shrewd irony, that many philosophers persist in regarding man as the centre of the universe centuries after Copernicus has proved that he is not.

An optimistic view of man leads to a belief in inevitable moral progress, a conviction that Hulme found not only disgusting, but also patently absurd. For, as he asks, what is the goal of such development? Progress and evolution were to him purely biological terms. Therefore he feels more attracted by *l'Action française* and its idea of classicism[49]. The movement was started by Charles Maurras in 1908, and in his book *L'Avenir de l'Intelligence* (1900) Maurras identified democracy with the death of politics, and Romanticism with the death of art.

Hulme is at pains to wriggle out of Sorel's ideas and his support to the people behind l'Action française. Still, he calls Sorel the most important socialist thinker since Marx[50] because he held that moral and heroic discipline is required in order to bridle man's innate wickedness. Hulme undoubtedly had Fascist leanings, but he is not so outspoken as Pound. However, it would be wide of the mark to call Hulme a democrat. In a general way he distrusted the common people's capacity to judge about things. He subsumed the problem under his beloved categorization general versus specific: the general – democracy as an ideal – might be acceptable, the specific ideas that the democratic movement is associated with are despicable. Here we see again Hulme's contrast between ideals and ideas. He emphatically refutes the conventional assumption that thinking in terms of democracy is a necessary paradigm[51], and he finds the ideology connected with the working classes false[52].

CHAPTER TEN

HULME'S LITERARY THEORIES

INTRODUCTION

In a passage in *Speculations*[1], Hulme says that architecture is the only art that moves him. He was probably thinking of the almost architectural sculptures of his friends Epstein and Gaudier-Brzeska, whose works lived up to Hulme's standards of hardness and dryness. Perhaps it was just an off-hand remark, for there are no descriptions of buildings in his oeuvre, and his theory of art refers only cursorily to architecture. But there are numerous comments on geometrical figures.

Hulme's theory of art includes literature, painting, and music. Music he calls "a fortuitous assemblage of noises"; and he suggests that the beats of a conductor's baton are related to the rhythm of the body (which is left unexplained)[2]. Music mainly interests him for its capacity to keep a crowd together like an organism[3]. It is his reflections on literature that take up most of the pages of what he wrote, even though his contemporaries thought that he was more interested in the visual arts than in poetry[4]. Perhaps we get closer to the truth if we suggest that he strove to establish a holistic structure of what was immaterial and spiritual. His favourite religious dogmas shine through his criticism.

Literature to Hulme means poetry; the novel and the drama receive virtually no attention. Most of his literary criticism appears in a few articles, eg *A Lecture on Modern Poetry*. His *Notes on Language and Style* is almost exclusively about poetry. The title is very appropriate: the presentation is abrupt and desultory, association being the structuring principle. The work seems to have been written in haste, or to be meant as a draft. Many of the pronouncements are inconclusive statements or *obiter dicta* that are not properly worked out. Even if Hulme's prose is seemingly straightforward and, unlike his poetry, not characterized by unexpected images, the lack of consistency and argumentation of the *Notes* sometimes makes the work heavy reading.

Hulme was himself aware of the problem: well into the *Notes*[5], he expresses his fear that "these remarks" should be somehow arranged in a system; in that case they would risk degenerating into commonplaces. In isolation, however, they may hopefully "suggest great unities". The formulation is symptomatic:

the 'great unities' – the toal overview – can be suggested in glimpses only. Understanding is unobtainable by the patient, long haul.

Hulme's literary criticism consists of many digressions. But he does not develop a coherent theory of literature or literary creation. He is generous with value judgments: literature is nothing new under the sun, a happy escape from platitude[6]; literature is the fact of standing still and getting a brief, artificial view[7], a characterization that fits literature into his Bergson-inspired philosophy: literature is a poise in the flux of life, and the view granted is artificial because literary works are artefacrts, not copies.

Hulme is firmly mounted on his anti-transcendentalist hobbyhorse: poetry is a means of communication[8]; poetry is direct communication, prose indirect[9]. Whereas poetry arrests the reader's mind with an image, prose allows his consciousness to continue towards a conclusion with the least possible effort[10] – a statement that is not meant to be positive. Hulme rejects the idea of the infinite out of hand (even though he is fond of some abstract Absolutes), and he takes a reviewer to task for saying that poetry causes the soul to soar to higher regions[11]. Prose uses dead images, but images are born in poetry[12]. So Hulme solves the centuries-old problem of how to distinguish between poetry and prose by looking at their respective use of images. The reason why he criticized late Victorian and contemporary poems was mainly that so many dead images occur in them.

Science and Poetry

In Hulme's opinion, literature fought science on its own ground, viz. the picture it gave of the world and the theories it propounded about truth. He was bitterly opposed to the idea that empirical knowledge is the whole of knowledge. Science has changed the world into a mechanical toy, but its pretensions to give a valid picture of 'things as they are' – Hulme never uses the word reality – is absurd, not least because it is hostile to religion. In the opening passages of the *Notes*, Hulme claims that poetry, not science, can reflect the unity of the world. Accordingly, the Renaissance is to him the great bugbear because it was during that period that the method of scientific enquiry began to dominate man's thinking. The two combatants, science and poetry, use the same medium, viz. language. Hulme asserted that hard and dry statements are not the preserve of science. Actually, hard and dry are two favourite terms of his in his description of the ideal poetical language.

Poetry sholud be neither introspective nor transcendent, neither sentimental nor narrative in the Aristotelian sense of having a beginning, a middle, and an end. The ideal is for poetry to be moderately didactic, mimetic without copying, and, above all, revelatory of the mundane because the poet's task is to show his readers something about 'reality' and 'truth' that no one else can do.

Hulme admits that poetry has sometimes erred: earlier it was a form of entertainment for 'warriors and bankers'[13]: it incited warriors and tickled the ephemeral caprices of a cultural elite, who might also use poetry in their love letters. And the Romanticists' gushing forth of their innermost feelings made him sick, as did the hollow ornateness of late 19th century poetry – incidentally the very period when science demonstrated the impact of a hard and dry terminology.

Modern poetry, however, ought to be aware of its function, viz. to create a plastic picture. Thus it becomes more reminiscent of sculpture than of music. The sculptor Gaudier-Brzeska talked about a sculptural conception of masses in relation, and the isolated, arresting images occurring in the poetry of the Imagists and Hulme were comparable to statues. As Hulme puts it, in modern poetry "the egg has broken its shell"[14]. In contrast, the 'old art', by which Hulme seems to mean Romantic and Victorian poetry, used the hypnotic effect of rhythm to influence the reader[15] "Poetry is neither more nor less that a mosaic of words", says Hulme[16]. If implemented, that theory tends to neglect the overall structure. Hulme does not see that as a danger, however, witness his repeated statement that the poem selects its own structure.

THE POET

Ford Madox Ford said, "I register my own time in terms of my own time". Hulme largely agreed. To him, the poet is neither a visionary nor a prophet, and yet he is more than the Wordsworthian "man speaking to men". The poet, like the painter, is a man who is able to comprehend the beauty potential of some objects[17]. But Hulme is unwilling to accept the idea of the poet as a human being holding mystical communion with the Infinite. He discards that Romantic thought as "a popular idea", which it requires too much effort to believe. The poet's personality is finite, yet he finds himself in a continuous struggle with something greater than himself[18]. The poet is a man who has a talent of marshalling isolated moments so as to produce "a mystic separation"[19] – between flux and poise, we are allowed to conclude.

The poet is a frail vessel because his state of gestation makes him vulnerable[20]. His activity requires concentration (Hulme uses the adjective 'tense'), and admits of no disturbance. But then again, writing poetry is a healthy pursuit, and the poet is serene because the process is beneficial to him. However, it may take some time before he acquires the ability to write: he has to "think in air", perhaps for years, before learning to exploit his capacity to think in terms of analogies[21].

The poet connects his discrete moments of ecstasy, presenting them, in the finished product, in great impersonal words as an image of a more valuable existence[22]. However, even if linked together, the moments preserve their idiosyncratic character, and the 'valuable existence' is not synonymous with 'a higher life'[23]. Hulme expressly denounces "literary men" for creating, or attempting to create, such a life. He calls it downright hypocrisy, saying that the expressions used on such occasions are big words without any personal meaning. Hulme does not specify what he means by "a more valuable existence"; all he says is that the isolated ecstasies demand anchoring in the mundane, for which reason the soul comes in handy[24].

The links do not seem to be immediately obvious here: the poet is a maker, but at the same time he is a kind of medium, and the soul is a necessary prerequiste. In this context, 'soul' is a sort of original talent enabling the poet to select some of the given sense impressions and to discard others, so as to produce an epiphany. But the soul is not the poet's prerogative, and Hulme admits that even the mob can be granted glimpses of the soul.

Hulme says that he came to poetry "from inside", because he was searching for a way to express "certain emotions". And emotion is unlike rhetoric in that it always has a physical starting-point[25]. Though his concern was personal, Hulme takes exception to egocentric and psychological poetry – that is what he calls "mere putting down"[26]. Using images and symbols to evoke magic is objectionable, for it means that you let infinity in through the back door. Hulme instances Yeats.

Hulme's poetry is personal in that it records his own sense impressions in what are, to him, appropriate illustrative analogies and equivalents. It is a *sine qua non* for poetic descriptions to express genuine involvement. However, his poetry is impersonal in the sense that he does not initiate his readers into his own problems, and he does not wear his heart upon his sleeve.

Literature and its Raw Materials

Literature is possible, says Hulme, echoing Aristotle[27]. It carries the reader into an artificial world. "My adjustment to the imaginary toy" leaves the basis of things unchanged. This latter point is worth emphasizing, for Hulme is a bit uncomfortable about "working in imaginary land", and he pays tribute to the down-to-earth farmer whose fields do not change under the influence of literature[28]. Literature gives us nothing new under the sun, but it is "a happy escape from platitudes «"[29]. Rugged realistic literature, as seen in eg Zola, is boring[30], and propagandistic or explicitly didactic writing is not literature in the true sense of the word.

The material of art is dead things and situations which we strive to put into words[31], but life contains lifts as well as gaps – there will invariably be intervening periods of listlessness where all a poet can do is to make use of commonplace language, or, to use Hulme's idiosyncratic terminology, "move counters"[32]. Hence his characterization of poetry as a conbination of creative moments and ready-made lines[33].

If we are to judge from his own poems, the raw material of literature can be widely different things: the sky, the sun, the moon, trees, but also housetops, girls, and marching armies. They are all sense impressions able to prompt emotions in him – which miners are not, for which reason he considers them less suitable as a poetical subject.

THE CREATIVE PROCESS

According to Baudelaire, inspiration is the same for all artists, irrespective of their medium[34]. Hulme's originality as a thinker consists in his hypothesis of the bipartition of the thinking process as such: image-making is postulated to be a constituent of thinking. The creative artist is distinguished from ordinary mortals in that his thought process works in terms of such parallels. The inspiration of the image-creating thought is, for Hulme, a sense impression; even a short and transitory impression is liable to be cultivated so as to become an emotion that is describable. Inspiration is "a matter of an accidentally seen analogy or unlooked-for resemblance"[35].

What is interesting is that it is not the object *per se,* but its – presumably intuitively grasped – analogical potentialities that trigger off poetic creation. When Hulme says that a poet's task is to see things as they are – a formulation that owes something to Matthew Arnold – he means things as they present themselves to his two-tier perception. The theory of the two-sidedness of a poet's mental activity makes it easier to understand the large number of dichotomies that we find in Hulme's critical oeuvre.

Hulme uses a peculiar word to describe the poet's state of mind before creation begins: he is "disillusioned", and so is the reader before becoming acquainted with the poem. 'Pre-illusioned' might seem to be a more appropriate term, for the two parties are at a stage before illusions are created – illusions that the reader subsequently believes in and appreciates even if he knows that they *are* illusions. But appreciation requires what Coleridge called "the willing suspension of disbelief".

The language, which Hulme looks upon as the dress of the thought ("the metaphor clothes the idea"[36]), naturally clings around and adjusts itself to the bifurcation. Effort is required on the poet's part: Hulme's analogy is the Biblical statement of a woman in labour. The thought can only be conveyed in terms of an analogy if language is to be faithful to the thought – and that happy combination is the hallmark of the poet.

Ideally speaking, the poet should make a plaster model of what he wants to express in order to be able to verbalize his emotional reaction to what he sees[37]. However, that might be difficult in some cases, for Hulme was also inspired by what he called "the lowest elements" or "street feelings", eg looking at shop windows, or seeing two prostitutes walking down Piccadilly[38]. It is not a matter of adding a mechanical layer of conventional ornamentation that is prompted more or less automatically, but a verbalization of an intuitive grasp of a resemblance.

The next stage is *contemplation*, as Hulme calls it. That is the process of licking the product into shape. Two familiar terms, used idiosyncratically by Hulme, come into the picture here: *invention* is the taking note of 'accidentally seen' analogies and arranging them in a certian order[39]. Invention, then, is a rational procedure referring to planning rather than to making up. *Intention*, in Hulme's idiolect means the choice of tone (eg narrative or emotinal) and form. That, too, seems to be a conscious operation. Both 'invention' and 'intention' are subordinate to 'contemplation'.

The stage that follows contemplation is called by Hulme *expression*. The poet begins with separate sentences, it seems – the artist's struggle to verbalize his sense impressions. Hulme stresses the need for the poet to make written notes so as to have some material for his later work. He has a very pertinent designation for untreated material, viz. *clay* – heavy, sticky soil that is susceptible of being shaped. The finished work will be a completely detached thing-in-itself. The movement in the creative process is from a *vision* to a *voice*. The end product is "the exact model analogy", ie an acoustic and linguistic rendering of the poet's sense impressions.

It is interesting that, like the 18th century theorists, Hulme should operate with a stepwise progression: he divides in order to be able to conquer. Even if they are not strictly compartmentalized, the stages are discernible. It is necessary for the artist to be detached from the requirements of everyday life because he has to "go into the field" (Hulme's formulation is borrowed from natural science) in order to experience the ecstacy that is the prerequisite of poetic creation. That state of 'standing outside ' (the literal meaning of 'ecstasy') is, as in Wordsworth's 'emotion recollected in tranquility' followed by a second stage of conscious reflection, or *clarification,* as Hulme calls it[40].

Poetry arises as a result of a great zest in the poet's contemplation of something[41]. The process takes some elbow grease and consumes considerable amounts of paper, for the poet's task is to formulate his individual vision in a language that normally serves to express conventional and ordinary perception[42]. Zest leads to accurate descriptions, and the goodness or badness of a poem is proportional to the amount of zest that went into the making of it[43].

For the poet to become "the transforming influence"[44], an ability to cast "a grid over oneself" is required[45]. In Hulme's formulation, it is difficult to dwell on a point when one wants to evoke an idea[46] – the 'point' being the image, and the 'idea' being the 'unities' lying behind. He uses the analogy of seeing things on the ground from a balloon. Objects that are conventionally viewed in utilitarian terms will suddenly appear in a non-utilitarian light if the angle is shifted.

Gradually, the poet will learn to establish what Hulme calls 'poises' in the current of life, and the poet will create his own 'chessboard', which enables him to play the language game, or "move the counters" (see pp. 113 et seq.)[47]. There is a kind of interplay between poet and poem: the poet creates the poem, but the poem, in its turn, selects and structures, shedding light on the poet's attitude and making it more definite for him[48]. From the chain of words, the poet gets a *new* picture (Hulme's italics). The original thought is transformed during the process, the search for form into which the individual sentences are to be fitted leads to the creation of new images - *creative* effort means *new* images (Hulme's italics)[49].

That is what explains Hulme's statement that "in a sense the poetry writes itself". He denies the intervention of any conscious intellecutal effort and talks about «creation by happy chance", comparable to a painter's accidental strokes of the brush. What Hulme has in mind is reminiscent of the Horatian *curiosa felicitas,* ie the fortunate formulation with which the talented poet is inexplicably favoured as a reward for his diligent labour. Hulme repeatedly emphasizes the significance of the accidental discovery; he does not develop the idea, but it is interesting in the light of eg. the Deconstructionists' assumption of the autonomy of language.

In moments of creation. Hulme says, the poet is comparable to a drunken person leaning on a table to support himself[50]: a state of intoxication will bless the poet with a vision of unity, and it will provide him with original as well as profound thoughts. That state gives him relaxation, and somehing will happen to his "inner psychology"[51]. Also religion and music can be instrumental in prompting creation; alcohol is, as Hulme puts it, "a supporting medium"[52]. He claims to be able to prove that some epiphanies have actually been brought about thanks to the influence of alcohol. In one of his few bursts of humour he adds drily that hence it must be obvious that epiphanies have nothing to do with a "higher world"[53]

Fancy and Imagination

Hulme deals with the two concepts in his great essay *Classical and Romantic*[54]. He starts by referring to Coleridge's ground-breaking distinction between them, but he does not go into a detailed explication of, or comment on, the terms, and he does not mention Coleridge's name.

To Coleridge, imagination is a spontaneous power of the mind that is deeply involved in the creative act, ie it was a mental phenomenon. But Hulme was suspicious of imagination because of the uncontrolled indulgences in it that had spoiled so much of 19th century poetry[55]. Hulme uses the term, but does not establish a clear-cut division of labour betwen fancy and imagination, the latter being to him a nondescript concept that somehow hovers behind or above fancy. Fancy is useful where the contemplation of concrete objects is concerned because it provides an analogy that "points beyond the thing"[56]. Fancy, then, is the metaphor-creating faculty, the instrument through which imagination manifests itself. However, what really makes fancy appeal to Hulme is the fact that it is associated with limitation[57]. Fancy can create something that a detailed analysis is capable of isolating or defining[58]. On the other hand Hulme also claims that imagination is involved "when the analogy gives an accurate description" so that "hard and dry" poems are produced[59].

Hulme's treatment of fancy and imagination is unsatisfactory – cursory and anything but clear. He seems to have only a nodding acquaintance with the terms, and he does not put the distinction to any real use. Hulme was suspicious of an Absolute like the Coleridgean imagination, and he had nothing new to contribute on the subject. It will be seen that in an important respect, viz. that of creating images, his fancy is identical with Coleridge's imagination.

The Subject

The greatnesss of a poem depends on the accuracy of the observation, not on the grandeur of the subject[60]. The subject plays an unobtrusive part; what matters is for the poet 'to see things as they are', and not as we have been taught to see them.

Old poetry was mostly about "heroic action". More modern, eg Romantic, poetry was mainly about the "the expression and communication of momentary phases of the poet's mind". Hulme detested such laying bare of one's soul. He discards "all books, history, etc." that are nothing but "artifical moments and poses of literary men"[61]. His grievance is that such authors do not 'see things as they are'- he cites Millet's romanticized painting of miners as a frightening example, and he deplores the fact that "other social classes" than literary men, eg peasants (mute inglorious Miltons?) are left inarticulate. A suitable subject for Hulme himself, he says, would be a fair-haired woman with upturned face in Regent Street in London[62].

The subjects of his poems are concrete to the point of being trivial. He deliberately avoided the Unknown of every kind. Characteristically, when he writes about potentially 'great' subjects, like the sun or the moon, they are not seen in a cosmic or mythological context, but are pulled closer to the earth, so to speak.

Mimesis

As is the case with so many other theoretical concepts, Hulme's treatment of mimesis is not unambiguous; in one passage he almost practises documentarism: "It began in the E.M. restaurant…"[63]. But on the following pages he distances himself from the French naturalists, eg Zola' "sordid pieces". Such imitation is "interminable, dreary, commonplace"[64], and he tartly remarks that if literature really did imitate life, warts and all, it would have to include detailed accounts of eg eating and dressing. He warns his fellow poets against the misunderstanding that the evocation of realistic details influences the reader favourably, however fond of them the poet himself may be. Turner was fascinated by locomotives, but he hid a railway train in steam because his instinct told him that "immediate precision" was undesirable[65].

When Hulme speaks of imitation, he means imitation of things, feelings, and situations, not the taking of literary predecessors as one's models. Many a bad poet is bad for the simple reason that he copies a great forerunner slavishly. But he does not make it clear to what extent imitation is justifiable. He only says that all literature has to select because there ought to be *new* (his italics) emotions in the poems, eg descriptions of flowers and "of infinitely fascinating men and women"[66]. Imitation risks becoming insipid for the very reason that it makes room for few, if any, novel emotions[67]. The potential beauty of cranes and chimneys is waiting to be evoked – such objects are "organized pieces of cinders"[68] (see pp. 113 et seq. about 'cinders').

Hulme acknowledges that art may in some cases create a kind of beauty that does not exist in nature; that is often the case in the pictorial arts, he says. But the situation is different when the medium is language: nature is rich, and words can only render a thin shadow – they are like a gramophone[69]. That is a telling illustration: the gramophone was a recent invention that was capable of giving a fairly accurate rendering of 'his master's voice', but which would invariably fall short when compared with a live performance. Hulme pursues the idea by saying that literature is not the deed in itself, but the shadow cast by the deed. This passage does not reflect Hulme's usual confidence in the power of language.

Mimesis was beside the point for a man of Hulme's inclination because it would invariably limit or curb the poet's image-creating faculty. What interested him was not true-to-life copies or gentle adaptations. His point lay elsewhere: striving for a new way to look at familiar things.

Form

Around 1912, prompted by Flint and Fletcher, Hulme began to study French poetry. He wrote an article in the August 1912 issue of *The Poetry Review* about French poetry since 1880. The gist of the article is a wish for English poetry to obtain the same formal liberty as French poetry had known for some years, and he argued that each age must produce its own verse form.

Hulme had some reservations vis-à-vis content because so much of Edwardian and Georgian poetry was concerned that "some vague mood shall be communicated"[70], ie content took pride of place. By the same token, the reason why he distrusted many of the "romantic jewels" was that they had become emptied of their poetical potential[71].

Hulme is preoccupied by the thorny question of form versus content. He tries to keep them separated, but cannot really make up his mind as to which of them is the more important, be it in the individual work or in the poetic expression of an age. He places the dichotomy in a larger context: he calls attention to the contrast between the Greeks' conception of the world as continuous movement and their desire to create something permanent and immortal. To underpin his assertion he cites Plato's doctrine of ideas. The Greeks were convinced that there was one perfect way to dress the thought, hence their elaborate rules of regular metre and their tendency to incorporate history and philosophy into their poetry[72].

Hulme uses the egg/shell metaphor to illustrate his point: modern poetry has changed its content, "the egg" has abandoned the ancient art of chanting, and accordingly "the shell" must be broken, ie the mechanism of verse must be altered[73]. That statement points to the primacy of content, as does his repeated insistence that form is dependent on the creation of new images. However, that assumption is at variance with his reflections on the way new art forms are created.

Hulme sees a connection between a verse form and the state of poetry in a given period[74]: when poetry flourishes, it is because a new verse form is discovered or introduced. The greatness of Elizabethan poetry was especially due to the importation of new forms from France and Italy[75], Thus, indirectly, he attempts to explain the 'reformation' of poetry in his own age by the adoption of new verse forms from France. However, his own poetical practice belies his formalist predilection: again and again in his reflections, it is the necessity of the striking image that comes to the fore. The question of metrical or non-metrical verse tends to recede into the background.

Hulme claims that new art forms "suddenly" come into existence: they are introduced deliberately by people who hate the old ones. New bottles create new wines, it seems. 'Suddenly' is a key word because it frees him of the obligation to consider 'developments', which he detested. The formulation appropriately describes what the Imagists did, and it may have some general validity. Thus Pope's adoption of the heroic couplet may to a great extent be explained by his contempt for the multiplicity and intricacy of the metres used by the Metaphysical poets. Hulme quotes with approval the French theorist Gustave Kahn, saying that the latter's ventures into uncharted waters with regard to *vers libre* were the fundamental cause of the renascence within contemporary French poetry.

Paradoxically, Hulme puts a biological grid over the issue of form, talking about the birth, life-cycle, and ultimate death of a verse form[76]. Forms die of wear and tear, it appears[77]. He instances the French 'Parnassiens', who were defeated by the marvellous felicity of a new form[78]. Every age must find a form of its own, ousting the others. It seems to be a matter of poetical Darwinism – the survival of the fittest. He has no doubt that the 'impressionism' of contemporary painting – he was very fond of Whistler's pictures- will soon find a formal equivalent within poetry, viz. free verse[79]. Look to France, he says: after the birth of the new form there has been a flourishing of marvellous poets.

Form gives the reader a sense of satisfaction by the skilful arrangement of the material. To Hulme, *vers libre* is not synonymous with a haphazard accumulation of words. The poet's "intention" is responsible for the creation of the form: he begins with some vague phrases and then gropes his way towards the form, like a painter or a composer. He admits that he had trouble finding a metrical equivalent for "the vision of a London street at midnight"[80].

Hulme refers to "a new verse form" which is free without being identical with *vers libre*[81]. He does not exemplify – a general weakness with him! – but only adds that he has not found a poet that he could use as a model: neither Dante nor Milton was able to give him what he was looking for[82]. Perhaps he is hinting at the empirical fact that stylistic tightening is conditioned by metrical freedom.

What really interests Hulme is the rhythm of a given form. His discussion of the problem of metre occurs in *A Lecture on Poetry:* the rhythm should be suitable to the picture evoked[83]. He is not blind to the difficulty of evoking an image and fitting the rhythm to the idea; on the other hand, the old regular metre "takes away all the trouble for us" and is incompatible with the delicate pattern of image and colour[84]. Regular metre covers a good deal of "imitative and sentimental poetry"[85], which accounts for his rejection of it.

On the whole, metrical verse is the arch enemy, and Hulme is generally suspicious of what he calls "old poetry" - indeed, he would willingly destroy all poetry that is more than 20 years old[86]. Old poetry not only strove to embody perfection of thought; more than that, it was meant to express "oracles and maxims", and it used metre "as a helpmate for the memory"[87]. Besides, it was possible for a poet to write metrical verse, even if there were holes in his poetical inspiration[88].

Old poetry is like the pyramids – "history in symbolic characters"[89]. It contained both history and philosophy, which necessitated elaborate rules about regular metres. But here Hulme seems to jump to conclusions; it is a bold and, it would seem, unwarranted leap in the argumentation: surely it would be possible to write a poem on a historical or philosophical subject without having to conform to intricate metrical patterns?

Old poetry was chanted, not read, for which reason a regular metre was mandatory[90]. However, modern poetry is certainly not meant to lull the reader asleep, but to "arrest the attention so much that the succession of visual images should exhaust one…Recording impressions by visual images…does not require the old metric system «[91], which would inevitably be felt as a Procrustes' bed. The new form is "clothes made to order, rather than ready-made clothes"[92], another instance of Hulme's talent of pithy formulation.

New poetry must appeal to the eye, like sculpture, it must "mould images… into definite shapes"[93], and , by implication, not indulge in vague romanticism. New poetry consists of a series of visual images that are combined, "a visual chord"[94].

Hulme's reflections on form, though convincing in some passages and never uninteresting, are inconclusive. The question of the harmony of verse does not interest him at all. And when he says that the primary aim of poetry is not a maximum of individual expression[95], he seems to have forgotten his own poetical practice, which shows a series of highly idiosyncratic observations – a natural consequence of his injunction to 'see things as they are'. His contrasting of metrical verse and free verse tends to become a crusade of freedom versus constraint, and he does not really get to grips with the form/content dichotomy, which has continued to be a moot point, even among the most prominent critics, to this day. And for all his criticism of 'old poetry', which remains a vague designation, never defined, exemplfied, nor placed in time, he admits that the content of poetry is based on tradition[96]. The conclusion would seem to be that the difference between old and new poetry is essentially one of form. And that means that form and content are separate entities.

Furthermore, it is a questionable assumption that pithy formulations and striking images are contingent on the use of a specific metre, witness Pope's heroic couplets, which abound in elegantly phrased *bons mots*. And, finally, it would be difficult to defend the position that the Romanticists got a new metre (which one?) sent from heaven and proceeded to adjust their 'matter' to it.

Language

Hulme's poetical ideal is "accurate, precise, and definite description"[97], which is what he understood by classicism. That is the way philosophy uses language, and philosophy is, to Hulme, to a very large extent a semantic discipline. Regrettably, his treatment of language and thought does not live up to his poetic ideal. It is not easy to follow because it contains more than a sprinkling of idiosyncracy and fogginess.

Language is based on, and subordinate to, nature, he says. 'Nature' is here to be taken in the restricted sense of 'country', that which is the opposite of 'town'. Hulme disliked the country and was annoyed that so many metaphors, even such as are used in philosophical parlance, ultimately derive from farmers' language. He postulates that language – but not thought – would have assumed a different shape if words had had their origin in a town context. He instances the word 'stream', which gives associations to a landscape scene.

Like Wittgenstein later, Hulme attacks the idea that 'meaning is', and that language is logical[98]. Also, he asserts that language and thought are separate, and he rejects the idea that there is a one-to-one correspondence between a thought and its formulation: it is possible to express a thought in several different ways. What he objects to in logic is that it prevents the free play of the image-making faculty: logical expression is equivalent to manipulating images[99].

I.A.Richards points to a peculiarity of language that is an apt illustration of

Hulme's problem: language is a completion and does what the intuitions of a sensation cannot do by themselves; words cannot hand over sensations bodily. Words are the meeting-point at which regions of experience that can never combine in sensation or intuition come together[100]. Hulme is far less theoretical, deploring the insufficiency of language in general terms and speaking disparagingly about "the connections in language" [101], and he compares a sentence to a crawling worm[102].

Since a word to Hulme is an image, a sequence of words is a sequence of images[103]. However, like Coleridge, he was aware that "no simile runs on all four legs", ie there is not a one-to-one correspondence between a figurative term and whatever you apply it to, for, as Abrams pertinently points out, otherwise you would not be able to realize that it *is* figurative[104]. But a string of words is not enough to create poetry, for words are physical entities, and in order to achieve his end, the poet must perform the art of the snake charmer. Hulme calls words "that curious rope of letters". The prose writer just drags meaning along with the words whereas the good poet raises the rope (hence the analogy of the snake charmer), beating the reader with it. The point is to make words "*stand up*"[105] (Hulme's italics).

However, the context within which words appear is of crucial importance, and almost imperceptibly Hulme slides from a concern with the individual word to an awareness of the significance of the larger unit. A word to him is a combination of a notional content and a syntactic function – even if he does not use those terms. The problem is that language has come to be used to serve a different kind of communication from that with which poetry is concerned. So the poet has to conjure up another meaning than the dictionary one. Hulme hates smoothness, by which he understands a use of language that is too slack to strike the reader[106]. But solidity, ie language based on ideas, is an asset[107]. Words that have lost their evocative power are compared to a tree that has become a mast[108], ie a living organism reduced to the status of a mere tool.

For the stage following upon words Hulme uses two terms, *phrase* and *sentence*. 'Phrase' is an ambiguous term in Hulme's usage. Sometimes it merely refers to a collection of counters[109] (for counters, see pp. 113 et seq.), but he also uses the term to cover more independent expressions and turns of speech. He stresses the importance for an aspiring writer to familiarize himself with "all possible phrases"[110]. A good procedure will be to learn a new word and some phrases every day[111], and reading a lot of material written in English will prove helpful[112].

Hulme mentions something he calls the sentence unit, but the difference between phrases and sentences does not become evident. He wishes he could establish a lexicon for sentences so that it would be easier for people to communicate in ordinary conversations. However, he is suspicious of sentences because of their linearity – the words do not 'stand up' in sentences, it seems. One last grievance is that, in the case of sentences, readers' reactions can hardly be remote-controlled in the way Hulme aspired to do with the individual image.

Hulme distinguishes between direct and conventional (or indirect) language[113]. Indirect language is prose, which consists of what in one passage he calls relics of dead poets' analogies. The raw material of direct language, that is to say poetry, is living images[114]. There is a clear difference between the communicative task and values of poetry and prose: if it is a matter of putting across "mere meaning", many ways are open, and any style will do[115]. However, if the poetical statement is successful, it will not leave the reader with many options (se pp. 117-18, the section called *The Reader*).

Cinders and Counters

Since, to Hulme, poetry was a mosaic of words, it is not surprising that he should focus on the function of the individual word. *Cinders* and *counters* are two words that are peculiar to Hulme's idiolect, metaphors taken from two different cognitive realms, counters being words, cinders being concepts *and* words. They are opposites, but not complementary, and they have a bearing on Hulme's understanding of expression and meaning, as well as of the poet's task.

Counters are words used as the small change of language, serviceable in every situation of practical communication. When used as counters, words are mainly or exclusively denotational, any possible connotations having been pushed into the background, or entirely left out of account.

A counter is a useful 'coin', having no inherent worth but only the value that convention ascribes to it. In this case, convention is established by the rules of the game called communication on an everyday level. In our everyday use of language, we replace meaning by words that we accept unreflectingly. A reader or listener will usually take a word as an X in algebra, without the meaning attached because the meaning arises only as the product of a context. However, that is unsatisfactory to Hulme, who sees "each word with an image sticking on to it, never a flat word passed over a board like a counter «[116]. The analogy between language and a chessboard occurs in other passages of Hulme's criticism, and it is appropriate to point out that the slightly younger Wittgenstein developed a theory of language as a game.

Counters, says Hulme in his great essay *Classical and Romantic*, are signs in mathematics and words in prose[117]. Their shape suited his purpose: they are round and smooth rather than hard and dry. Each word has begun as a metaphor. But gradually it loses all meaning, "becoming a counter"[118]. Thus prose becomes a museum for dead metaphors, but poetry creates new phrases that are gradually taken over by prose. Today the expression "the hill was clad with trees" is felt as a factual statement; but the first time it was used, it was an image, a comparison with the clothes a human being wears[119]. In expositional writing, the connections have only counter value, which gives the presentation a pale, cliché-like quality. Hulme detested clichés because they are hackneyed or faded expressions that have been bantered about so frequently that they have lost their capacity of being "inflamed".

One type of prose finds favour in Hulme's eyes, viz. what he calls firm, simple prose. In such writing, counters may become valuable and acquire an inherent interest[120]. He is prepared to admit that language must necessarily contain many connections indicating precise relations[121]. Yet he looks askance at reasoning, for it is nothing but "arranging counters on the flat"[122], and logic is brushed aside as mere "counter pushing"[123]. In poetry, however, each word must be "an image seen, not a counter"[124], and there must not be any slack 'bridges' between the words[125].

That ideal is unattainable unless poems are very short, which Hulme's and the Imagists' are. And even though an unbroken succession of 'images seen' stands the very real risk of exhausting the reader, Hulme perseveres, nothing daunted: prose just takes the reader along, heading towards a conclusion[126]. Clear, logical expression must be banned from poetry because it confines the poet to "the use of flat, counter images only"[127].

Of course the poet has initially to work with counters, but he must create his own chessboard[128]. Thus he becomes a maker, the etymological meaning of the word poet. But he also influences the counters on the reader's chessboard. The poet is characterized by having a power over counters that the average man does not have: the latter's chessboard remains flat until it is activated and inspired by a poet. The moving of the counters is not without problems, for many people will find new angles of approach awkward, and the poet's procedure rough. Again we see that, in spite of his insistent disclaimers, there is an element of didacticism in Hulme's criticism: the reader must be taught, even disciplined.

Cinders have a burning potential that can be activated by competent handling. A possible source of inspiration for the name and the idea may be Bergson's *Évolution créatrice*, which suggests that inert matter is transformed into organisms because consciousness illuminates (*illumine*) it[129]. Ultimately, the idea harks back to Aristotle (whom Hulme does not mention), who maintained that matter has an embedded form. The poet can 'awaken' that dormant form, and Hulme's point is that awareness of the sleeping form can also be awakened in the reader.

The word 'cinders' is sometimes used to denote concepts. Thus Hulme declares that cinders are the criteria for all philosophical and aesthetic judgements[130]. But cinders are also the unorganised part of the cosmos[131]. In the hands of a competent poet, however, that chaos can be made to 'burn', ie become alive and structured. Poets, then, are instrumental in transforming nothing into something – a huge responsibility lies on their shoulders. Writing ought to be "a cindery thing", and life is "a gradual shifting of cinders"[132]. One of Hulme's favourite images, viz. the red dancer on a stage, is a built-up complex of cinders – hence her redness. Cinders are the glowing embers that are the foundations of our judgements[133]. Hulme hypothesizes a structure where cinders are the basis, and religion and judgement the superstructure.

In Hulme's discussion of cinders and counters much hinges on the question of expression. There should be a precise relation between "the inside image" and the form, ie expression. Analogies are capable of activating cinders, and the successful metaphor has acquired cindery qualities when verbalized. To be of real value, expression should be cinders-like.

Hulme's objection to scientific usage is that it reduces cinders to counters[134], or, to put it differently, it deprives the world of a valuable dimension. Something is lost in generalizations, yet he considers it an illusion to believe that the cindery world can be exactly represented by counters. If that were the case, the resulting counters would be very abstract, and, for the philosopher as well as for the poet, complete detachment from the world of empty counters is impossible.

Of course there is a certain amount of similarity between the mathematician's use of exact terminology and Hulme's repeated insistence on the "hard, definite" word[135]. But unlike the mathematician, whose use is strictly denotative, Hulme is concerned with the precise evocative effect of the words he uses. Characteristically and 'un-mathematically', in the quotation given a few lines above ("hard, definite"), there occurs a third adjective, viz. "personal" - the poet must know how to turn the tools of his trade to account.

Hulme's indignation was aroused by the fact that "at the present time" potentially cindery words like God and Truth are bandied about with very limited content and utterly "incapable of encompassing the world". Hulme finds that situation catastrophic and insists that at least some of the dignity of a cinder should be given back to such words – even if, he hastens to add, they are of course not reducible to mere cinders[136]. As could be expected, Hulme does not mince matters: there is too much empty talk in books about eg Life, Science, and Religion – "the kind of talk one could do if one wished". The good author, however, is the man who moulds "real clay", and whose style is "fire struck between stones"[137]. And, ultimately, if the world of cinders were to be reduced to "some few perfect counters", the result would be "an ungrit-like picture of reality"[138], a thought that filled Hulme with horror.

Hulme's achievement was to show that everyday, traditionally 'non-poetic' words (ie counters) like ships' masts can, in a specific context, acquire cinder status: a counter word can be 'heightened' by a poet who is worthy of the name. Conversely, words that are by convention felt to be 'natural' cinders, like sunsets, are put to multifarious irreverential uses by Hulme. There are no rules for the treatment of the ingredients of his poems, for which reason the concept of 'poetic diction' is *terra incognita* to him. His theory is that poetry necessitates a certain *use* of words, not a certain *category* of words.

Admittedly, Hulme's use of the terms counters and cinders is at times sloppy: counter is sometimes used in a neutral sense, but most often it is negatively loaded. By the same token, the ontological status of cinders remains obscure. But that should not be allowed to overshadow the fact that the gist of Hulme's reflections is of fundamental significance: poetry is a matter of the poet's handling of language; poetry uses language as a means, but also as an end. Traditionally, poems, like literature in general, 'are about' something. That applies to most of Hulme's poems too, even if they cannot be called narrative: two girls walking down Piccadilly, or a gentleman slipping on the pavement of the Embankment. The point is, however, that those situations – like others in Hulme's poems – become vehicles for an image, so that in a sense it can be said that the image is the subject of the poem.

Poetry appealed to Hulme, not least because his speculations on cinders are in accordance with his suspicion of infinity and limitlessness. The point for him is that cosmos is created out of a cindery chaos, and cosmos is somthing that is provided with structure and form. The poet can create beauty by organizing the pieces of cinders that are found in nature, and nature to Hulme means anything that is 'outside' man, for he exemplifies his idea of beauty as system with cranes and chimneys[139]– incidentally two frequently occurring motifs in his poems.

The objects of the world are done genuine justice to only when they are made to 'burn'. If that process were carried through, the world would come to look different from what appeared to an eye that was trammelled by convention. The world, then, is not a 'given', but something that is determined by the beholder's stance.

The Function of the Image

"The essential, fundamental element of the creative imagination…is the capacity of thinking by analogy, that is, by partial, and often accidental, resemblance", says the French critic Ribot in his *Essay on the Creative Imagiantion*[140]. No wonder that Ribot's theories had a great influence on Hulme and the Imagists. Hulme went one step further and asserted that a true poet's thinking cannot help proceeding in terms of analogies. Ribot also said that the subject of poetry is of minor importance. Also Taine saw the image, which he calls *métaphore,* as a help towards concrete representation, and not as a revealer of mystic relationships[141].

In his criticism of poetry, Hulme uses the word *analogy* as an umbrella term for what we would call analogy, image, and metaphor; but whereas Taine saw the analogy as a mask to disfigure (*travestir*) reality, Hulme thought that the analogy served to give a more precise picture of reality. Hulme could not accept a one-dimensional description that would leave it to the reader to catch sight of the analogy. To him a word is "a board with an image or statue on it"[142]. As mentioned earlier, in another passage Hulme said that the poet should make a plaster model when he began to write. The point for the poet is to convey the 'statue' to somebody else. It is the analogy that gives language its dynamism.

Analogies "make an other-world-through-the glass effect, which is what I want"[143]. Poetry is different from what we call reality, it is "life seen in a mirror"[144]. The idea of poetry as a means of making man one with the world did not appeal to Hulme at all. "It is the physical analogies that hold me…not the *vain*, decorative and verbal images of ordinary poets"[145]. The point of the analogy is to make the reader linger at "a point of excitement", ie to give him a thrill. Hulme illustrates his point with a parallel from streets: there are several categories of streets; some – the big routes – are characterized by movement; others – "the meeting-places" - by rest. The 'meeting-places' he calls "secular churches", where it is possible for a person to seek refuge and recharge his batteries. The mood is comparable to that which can be obtained in churches and theatres[146].

The Reader

The reader is the third panel of the triptych, the two others being the poet and the poem. Hulme does not distinguish between categories of readers, but lumps them all together, using the generic singular in his – to some extent unwarranted – optimism in dealing with the recipient of a poem.

Hulme is in accordance with the terminology within the psychology that was prevalent in his own day when he claims that the artist is capable of appealing to one or more layers of our Deep Self, and that there is an "original mood in our minds". The 'deep self' idea derives from Bergson, and its ontological status is dubious. Hulme does not explain what the mood is, or how it came to be located where it is supposed to be. His starting-point is that the reader may be able to see things, but is incapable of expressing them – yet, at the same time, he feels a need of having them expressed. The reader, then, has a potential that can be activated by the poet; there is a 'cindery quality' about the reader. As will be seen, Hulme comes very close to attributing to the reader the 'literary competence' that has been discussed by 20th century critics.

The difference between poet and reader is actually minimal since they are both able to give form to what is formless. What distinguishes the former from the latter is that, in that joint partnership, it is the poet that takens the initiative, and the reader responds emphathetically – he is "overpowered"[147]. The poet is the Voice, but Hulme's reflections are thought-provoking and modern because of the confidence he shows the reader and the responsibility he places on the reader's shoulders: he is the poet's opposite number, and active cooperation on his part is necessary if the artist is to achieve his aim. And Hulme goes a step further: he assumes that some privileged few among the readers are inspired by a successful poem "to make the same effort ourselves by rhythmical arrangement of words"[148]: poetry that has the intended effect prompts potential or budding poets to emulate their models.

The Objective Correlative

To Hulme, the most important aspect of poetic technique is the finding of a linguistic equivalent of a sense impression or a thought. The successful poem is "the exact model analogy" of the original impression[149]. The analogy idea was a current one: Gaudier-Brzeska saw the work as an abstraction of the artist's intense feeling, and Pound said that poetry gives us an equation for human emotion. Hulme admits that the problem is not always easy to solve – what, for example, is 'the exact model analogy' of two prostitutes walking down Piccadilly?

One inevitable corollary of the dictum is the necessity of verbal precision and economy; Hulme's own poems provide a rich collection of samples. In his application, the theory becomes an attempt to give poetry a quasi-scientific exactitude, perhaps in order to enhance its prestige. However, in Hulme's view, such increased precision is undertaken not least for the benefit of the reader. A poet had only performed his task satisfactorily to the extent that he could make the reader re-live the experience the poet himself had had. "The essential emotion is the excitement which is generated by direct communication" (sc. between poet and reader)[150]. If he is to succeed, it is not enough for the poet to inform the reader of the experience he has had and the concomitant emotion. Nor does a mere description suffice.

The poet's feeling should not be verbalized but conveyed as an image or a situation identical with, and expressive of, the poet's emotion. Of course the poem should please the receiver, but is should also make his reaction coalesce with that of the sender of the message. Thus the poet considers the *prodesse* as well as the *delectare* aspect, the instruction consisting in increased awareness on the reader's part.

Hulme's masterly poem *A Tall Woman* is a successful illustration of his aim: the movement in the poem is from calm to change and goes via illusion and disillusion to quasi-seduction. The woman is characterized, but not criticized. The only adjective used about her is the 'tall' of the title, but her tactics are unmistakably revealed. The reader will have no difficulty in identifying the poet's reaction: mild resignation vis-à-vis the superficiality of the woman's flirting. The changing situations isolate a feeling without mentioning its name.

> Solid and peaceful is Horton town
> Known is all friendship and steady.
> In fixed roads walks every man.
>
> A tall woman is come to Horton town…
> In the midst of all men, secretly she presses my hand.
> When all are looking, she seems to promise.
> There is a secret garden
> And a cool stream…
> Thus at all men she looks.
> The same promise to many eyes.
> Yet, when she forward leans, in a room,
> And by seeming accident her breasts brush against me,
> Then is the axle of the world twisted.

Hulme's emphasis on the reader's reception of a poem anticipates T.S.Eliot's theory about 'the objective correlative' down to the smallest dertail. A critic has defined Eliot's concept in the following way: "The objective correlative is a set of words, usually an image, so constituted that it produces in the reader a mental state which is as close as possible to that of the poet when he had the experience"[151]. Hulme himself puts it like this: "The artist makes me" (ie the reader) "realize a given object with his" (ie the artist's) "intensity"[152]

It can be argued that the demands made on the recipient of a poem are analogous to those made by a composer on the performer of his music in terms of speed and intensity. To do justice to the composer's work, you have to obey his directions. A correct interpretation does not deviate significantly from what the composer wrote on the sheet of music. That leaves limited scope for 'personal' approaches.

However, in the case of poetry, the issue is problematic. Of course a poet will write in order to have his poems read, but Hulme's attitude is binding on the reader in so far as it railroads his reactions and, by that very fact, deprives him of his freedom. For even if the theory is, superficially, reader-oriented, it is really an expression of the poet's hegemony, and neither Hulme nor Eliot gives an explanation of *why* identity of reaction is desirable.

The theory testifies to the power that is attributed to language: the poet neutralizes his own emotion and projects it on to the reader without mentioning it by name. The poem becomes an emotion-free link between identical feelings in poet and reader, as Murray Krieger puts it[153].

The one-to-one correspondence that is postulated between a given image and a given response works most smoothly in the case of simple, uncomplicated feelings like love, fear, or erotic obsession. Incidentally, those feelings are favourite themes in Hulme's poems. However, complex emotions, eg like those felt by soldiers marching off to war (the situation in one of Hulme's poems) are considerably more difficult to 'objectivize'. As a matter of fact, some of his poems are ambiguous as far as the objective correlative is concerned – which does not mean that they are bad poems.

Besides, there is a lot of evidence to suggest that readers can have idiosyncratic, yet valuable experiences with a text although their understanding of it does not tally with the writer's avowed intention. That is the reason why Derrida was so violently opposed to the idea: language has powers that we cannot control, he said, and the poet's personal vision may be apprehended entirely differently by a reader. Hulme ignores that problem completely, and Eliot, who was aware of the difficulty, side-tracked the discussion by insisting that that "does not diminish in the least the poet's responsibility to centre on the specific and distinct"[154].

The implication of the hypothesis is that there is an Ideal Reader or Group of Readers, even though their qualifications are never specified. Not is it made clear whether the required receptiveness is, or should be, different for works from different periods or genres. Perhaps Hulme and others supposed that the 'deeper self' in all human beings would ensure some degree of uniformity among readers.

Hulme's and other poets' frequent return to the reader's reaction anticipates the role that Barthes and reader response criticism award the reader. They go further than Hulme in the elimination of the author and leave all decisions regarding interpretation to something they call an 'interpretative community', whose characteristics are unfortunately never described. Thus the door is opened to a host of interpretations that are postulated to have the same validity – at least in principle. But Hulme and the Imagists were poles apart from that attitude. However, even if in their clubs and at their *soirées* they discussed their own poems and read aloud from them, there are no examples on record that they tested the validity of the theory of the objective correlative on each other.

CHAPTER ELEVEN

HULME'S POEMS

INTRODUCTION

Hulme was not quite satisfied with his own poems; he became increasingly suspicious of such "false categorizations of language"[1]. He would spend hours to find the exact formulation, and some of his instances of revision showed that he worked conscientiously with them to obtain maximum effect: thus *Sunset II* is more 'hard and dry' than *Sunset*. His painstaking efforts may be another reason why his output became so modest.

Sunset

I love not the Summer
That spréad like a scarlet sóre
O'er hálf sickly sky,
Or flaunts a tráiled red robe
Along the fretted edge of the city's roofs
Abóut the time of hómeward going crowds
Calling alóud for all to gápe
At its beáuty
Like a wánton.

But sunsets
When the sún comes hóme
As a shíp from the séa
With its round red sáil
Shádowed sharp against the dárkening sky
Quiet – in a cóol harbour
At eve
After wórk

(The accents are Hulme's – probably meant as advice to a reader of the poem as to how to scan the lines).

Sunset II

I love not the Sunset
That flaunts like a scarlet sore
O'er half a sickly sky,
That calls aloud for all to gape
At its beauty
Like a wanton.

But Sunset when the sun comes home
Like a ship from the sea
With its round red sail
Shadowed against a clear sky,
Silent, in a cool harbour
At eve
After labour.

Hulme left about 25 poems, totalling approximately 260 lines, to which should be added some *Images* consisting of one to four lines, not all of them classifiable as poems. The poems were probably written over a short period of years preceding their publication. Hynes suggests that the greater part were written during the years 1908-1910. Hulme never saw his own poems through the press.

In accordance with his poetical theory, Hulme's poems do not express feelings, but are almost clinical observations, precise descriptions of visible things; they are neither narrative nor didactic, but they could, with some justification., be called dramatic: a situation is 'performed' and 'pictorialized', but 'frozen' before being brought to a conclusion. As could be expected in the light of his objective correlative theory, Hulme says nothing explicit about the impact of the sense impressions – he passes the ball on to the reader, so to speak. Since they are essentially made up of his own associations, it would not be misleading to call the poems interior monologues.

Themes

The overriding theme of Hulme's poems is an alternative view of the world and, by inference, of the human condition. His poems express the comparability, indeed harmony, between the infinitely great (heavenly bodies) and the very small and down-to-earth (street scenes). The alternative view is propounded in its own right, but also as a criticism of science for its measurements of temperatures and distances, and of Romanticism for its use of heavenly bodies as mysterious and inaccessible deities.

As an example, we may look at Hulme's fondness for describing sunsets. A scientist would regard a sunset as a purely physical phenomenon and dwell on the spectrum of colours or see it as an exemplification of a cosmic cycle. Hulme chose sunsets because, in their light, 'reality' took on a different appearance from broad daylight. The subdued and soft light, the hues and shades with their suggestive potential, are as valid as an exact scientific statement about the phenomenon. And sunset is the time when ordinary people plod their way home from work.

Hulme does not pretend that there is one alternative 'truth'. His numerous revisions and the apparent inconsistencies we find as some of his poems go along are evidence that even limited aspects of reality cannot be adequately rendered by one image.

A pervasive theme is what may be subsumed under the heading *decline:* sunset, autumn, frustrated love, fading beauty. Love scenes are almost stills, not consummated, and the rich splendour of sunset is tinged with melancholy. In the light of his predilection for limitation and his disgust of Romantic flights of the imagination, it is paradoxical that quite a number of his poems should express hopes or dreams about physical removal – a kind of longing to escape into something unfamiliar and undefined. However, since the sitation is frozen, the aspirations are foiled.

Another dominant theme is explicit and implicit eroticism. In the poem *Town Sky-Line* everything is seen in terms of a woman's body; thus, the goddess of flowers lifts her gown so that her petticoat becomes visible. The chimneys are the tools enabling the narrator to peep under her skirt:

> On a summer day, in Town
> Where chimneys fret the cumuli,
> Flora passing in disdain
> Lifts her flounced blue gown, the sky.
> So I see her white cloud petticoat,
> Clear Valenciennes, meshed by twisted cowls
> Rent by tall chimneys, torn lace, frayed and fissured.

Celestial bodies often figure in potentially erotic situations: in *A Sudden Secret*, sea and water make cautious advances to a landscape, which, as in an 18th century landscape poem, is compared to the body of a sleeping woman. Consummation is discreetly and humorously conveyed:

> A sudden secret cove by Budley
> Waveless water, cliff enclosed.
> A stilled boudoir of the sea, which
> In the noon-heat lolls in to sleep.
>
> Velvet sand, smooth as the rounded thigh
> Of the Lady of Avé, as asleep she lay.
> Vibrant noon-heat, trembling at the view.
> Oh eager page1 Oh velvet sand!
> Tremulous faint-hearted waves creep up
> Diffident – ah, how wondering!
> Trembling and drawing back.
>
> Be bold – the Abbé blesses – 'tis only feignéd sleep.
> Oh smooth round thigh!...
>
> A rough wind rises, dark cliffs stare down
> Sour-faced Calvin – art thou whining still?

Often the narrator of a poem will hide his sexually tinted inquistitiveness behind names of costly fabrics and precious stones, and what has come to be recognized as Freudian symbols, viz. chimneys, masts, and tall trees, figure prominently in his poetry.

Women are a clearly felt reality to the narrator of the poems, who often plays the part of a Peeping Tom. Women are seen in terms of their sexuality, either as prostitutes with painted faces or as enticing temptresses with inscrutable smiles – but never as demure damsels. It is a well-known fact that Hulme was a sexually very active person and that he often treated women in a way that cannot be called gentlemanlike.

Natura naturata is never there in its own right; nature scenes are always meant to illustrate something else, and nature serves as the backdrop to the situation described in the poem. Considering the fact that Hulme was a deeply religious man, it is remarkable that only two of his poems deal with religion, and one of them, *Conversion*, is an emblem of any change from one creed to another, emphasizing the mood of uncertainty in the prospective convert before the decisive step is taken. The Christian religion is only indirectly alluded to, and the poem is an illustration of 'non-consummation' in that it deals only with the 'before' stage, ie the preparedness of the mind, and not the 'after' stage, ie the possession of the jewel of faith:

Light-hearted I walked into the valley wood
In the time of hyacinths,
Till beauty like a scented cloth
Cast over, stifled me, I was bound
Motionless and faint of breath
By loveliness that is her own eunuch.
Now pass I to the final river
Ignominiously, in a sack, without sound,
As any peeping Turk to the Bosphorus.

Composition

The Man in the Crow's Nest
(Look-out Man)

Strange to me, sounds the wind that blows
By the masthead, in the lonely night
Maybe 'tis the sea whistling – feigning joy
To hide its fright
Like a village boy
That trembling past the churchyard goes.

This text is characteristic of the way Hulme constructs many of his poems: a commonplace opening, a simple sensation, is followed by an image that is a parallel, or an extension, of the first observation. But what begins as the strange sounds of the wind develops into an anthropomorphic ascription of fear to the sea. Hulme tricks his readers by seeming to hold out to them prospects of one thing, and then proceeds to give them something entirely different. To use his own termninology, what begins as a 'counter' ends up as a 'cinder'. The 'here-and-now' situation is lifted out of time, so to speak, acquiring increasing depth, and the title of the poem says very little about the content.

In Hulme's poems there is a general situation that is subsequently illustrated, and in the process slightly changed, by one or more images. Hulme knew how to exploit what Lessing called ' the pregnant moment', and the stasis and matter-of-factness are further underlined by the significant absence of finite verbs, and the frequent occurrence of past and present participle constructions. Hynes talks about 'the principle of paratactical building blocks'[2]. The world emerging from Hulme's poems is a 'predicative' one: a substance is provided with attributes.

The element of contrast is an important structuring principle: the effect of stasis is counteracted by the succession of images used to illustrate the situation. Hulme's poems could be called polyphonic. There is a connection between the universe and man – in *The Man in the Crow's Nest* (see above) the sea is scared like a little boy, and in *Sunset II* (cf. p. 124) there is an opposition between the type of sunset that the narrator likes and one that he emphatically dislikes. By the same token, in virtually all Hulme's poems there is a clearly felt contrast between the nakedness of the description and the increasing suggestiveness of the image as we read the poem. His poems make a world come into existence before our eyes.

Hulme's tactic is to use a bifurcation of the reference of the image. The last line of *A City Sunset* unites two implications: "a vain maid loth to go" may be the lingering sunset as well as one girl in the crowd who refuses to leave the scene because she wants to benefit from the last rays of the sun. In the poem, the sunset can be a seductive woman as well as a concrete physical phenomenon that disturbs people on their way home with their erotically tinted fantasies:

> Alluring, Earth seducing, with high conceits
> Is the sunset that reigns
> At the end of westward streets…
> A sudden flaring sky
> Troubling strangely the passer-by
> With visions, alien to long streets of Cytherea
> Or the smooth flesh of Lady Castlemaine…
> A frolic of crimson
> Is the spreading glory of the sky,
> Heaven's jocund maid
> flaunting a trailed red robe
> along the fretted city roofs
> about the time of homeward going crowds
> -a vain maid, lingering, loth to go…

(The dots in this poem as well as the other poems quoted are Hulme's, and they do not indicate that something has been left out).

Form

Since most of Hulme's poems are very short (8-12 lines), the problem of stanzaic division is virtually non-existent. In the few cases where stanzas do occur, they are usually of uneven length, following the development of the description given in the text.

Rhymes are not a regular feature of the poems. *Above the Dock* is the only one whose four lines have a regular rhyme scheme (a,a,b,b):

> Above the quiet dock in midnight,
> Tangled in the tall mast's corded height,
> Hangs the moon. What seemed so far away
> Is but a child's balloon, forgotten after play.

Such rhymes as do appear in the other poems are distributed at random. The lines of the poems are of unequal length. A simple pattern is for one line to contain one item of information, or to coincide with a breath group. Consequently, the reader will not have to do violence to his pronunciation in order to make the words fit into a pre-established pattern. We actually have a manuscript in which Hulme has carefully marked the accents[3]. The speech rhythm is unimpeded, and Hulme uses practically no rhetorical devices.

Vocabulary

Hulme is able to use simple words both about his sources of inspiration (sea, trees, moon) and the figurative or image effect: he conquers his childhood fear of the moon by calling it a balloon, and *In the City Square* he describes the march of some soldiers (including the narrator) towards an unknown destination. The poem is a small epic of disillusionment – the soldiers soon become aware of the futility of their enterprise – but there is no sentimentality or more or less abstruse philosophizing. The two final words , which make up one line, are a suitable climax:

> In the city square at night, the meeting of the torches.
> The start of the great march,
> The cries, the cheers, the parting.
> Marching in an order
> Through the familiar streets,
> Through friends for the last time seen,
> Marching with torches.
>
> Over the hill summit,
> The moon and the moor,

> And we marching alone.
> The torches are out.
>
> On the cold hill,
> The cheers of the warrior dead
> (For the first time re-seen)
> Marching in an order
> To where?

Poetic diction is absent from his poems, but there are occasional quotations from, or references to, classical literature and the Bible. *Mana Aboda* describes a girl's annoyance that men just sing her praises instead of mounting her – they are "Josephs all", a reference to Genesis XXXIX, where we are told that Joseph in Potifar's house was not to be seduced from his continence, even by the sweetest of temptations:

> Mana Aboda, whose bent form
> The sky in achéd circle is,
> Seems ever for an unknown grief to mourn.
> Yet on a day I heard her cry:
> 'I weary of the roses and the singing poets –
> Josephs all, not tall enough to try'.

The fact that eroticism is an important theme of Hulme's poetry does not mean that his choice of words is in any way obscene. The erotic thrust is conveyed purely in terms of imagery, as is illustrated by, for example, *Far Back There:* the pool in the wood with the "tense, expectant surface" is waiting for its lover, "the ecstatic wave that ripples it/In sacrament of union". Again, consummation is discreetly hinted:

> Far back there is a round pool
> Where trees reflected make sad memory,
> Whose tense expectant surface waits
> The ecstacic wave that ripples it
> In sacrament of union,
> The fugitive bliss that comes with the read tear
> The falls from the middle-aged princess
> (Sister to the princely Frog)
> While she leans tranced in a dreamy curve,
> As a drowsy wail in an Eastern song.

Characters

Hulme's poems present a subject or a situation to the reader, who is subtly invited to observe and respond. They are not introspective or speculative, but 'directed outward', so to speak. Like Einstein, Hulme demonstrates that 'reality' is shaped by the interaction of two bodies, the observer and what is observed: reality is, ultimately, a subjective phenomenon. His poems give the reader a clear sense of the distinction between someone who beholds and something that is being beheld. There is always a narrator, sometimes explicitly there, as in one of the *Images:*

>I lie alone in the little valley, in the noon heat
>In the kingdom of little sounds.
>The hot air whispers lasciviously.
>The larks sings like the sound of distant
>Unattainable brooks.

Sometimes the narrator's identity is implied; the narrator of *Madman* seems to be the madman:

>As I walk by the river
>Those who have not yet withdrawn pass me
>I see past them, touch them.
>And in the distance, over the water,
>Far from the lights, I see the Night, that dark savage,
>But I will not fear him.
>Four walls are round me.
>I can touch them.
>If I die, I can float by.
>Moan and hum and remember the sea
>In heaven, oh my spirit,
>Remember the sea and its moaning
>Hum in the presence of God, it will sustain you
>Again I am cold, as after weeping.
>And I tremble – but there is no wind

A similar fluctuating treatment of the I-person is found in much contemporary literature, eg in Proust, whose *A la recherche du temps perdu* began to appear in 1913. The I-person of Hulme's poems is rarely there to tell a story; he presents an observation without explicating his own reaction to it.

The observer is physically inactive and always anonymous and nondescript. In most of his poems there are men and women who, though caught as in a photo snapshot, are engaged in some kind of action or movement – walking in a wood, creeping along the ground, or making erotic advances. However, motion is seen against a backdrop of stability. Objects and phenomena, as well as characters, are there in their wonted capacities. Trees are trees, and they do not suddenly begin to speak or reflect. Only, the prism that Hulme uses necessitates some willing suspension of disbelief on the reader's part.

IMAGES

Wittgenstein strove to transform logical innocence into logical awareness[4]:"There is enormously much added in thought to each proposition not said"[5]. He endeavoured to rectify the vagueness of ordinary propositions because he found that the vagueness was rectifiable. In the same way, Hulme aimed at changing visual and conceptual innocence into visual and conceptual awareness. As a matter of fact, the words 'image' and 'imagery' are misnomers since the primary appeal is not to the eye, but to the understanding. Hulme's purpose was also to rectify the vagueness of the conventional linguistic rendering of sensual experiences and give it hardness and dryness. He used images to show more than language can say - the image enunciates more than the linguistic formulation superficially seems to contain: he 'says' by showing because the image conveys a precision that is unobtainable by language.

Hulme's imagery is 'pure' in the sense that his images are not 'really' symbols; they are intended to bring about added insight, or to create a mood. Each of his poems contains at least one striking image —indeed, the image or images are the *raison d'être* of the poem, to which everything else is subservient. According to Aristotle, a good metaphor implies "an intuitive perception of the similarity in dissimilars, and the making of good metaphors requires an eye for resemblances"[6].. Metaphors are useful in cases where ordinary language seems deficient. The advantage of metaphor, as pointed out by Nowottny[7] is that it is possible to make a complex statement without a corresponding complication of the grammatical construction. The metaphor leads us to the meaning via the literal term - it is a 'non-linear demonstration'.

In order for people to understand literal meanings, Searle postulates the existence of something he calls 'background' in the minds of human beings: "Semantic content only functions against a background that consists of cultural and biological know-how which enables us to understand literal meanings"[8].

The situation is analogous where metaphors are concerned: in order for them to be effective and comprehensible, there must be what Max Black calls "a system of associated commonplaces"⁹. If we are to understand the metaphor 'man is a wolf', it is necessary to know the dictionary meaning of the word 'wolf' plus the responses made to the animal by people of any given culture. The commonplaces need not be true, but the essential thing is that they are freely and readily evoked.

The whole point of metaphor is that it is not normally possible: man is *not* a wolf. The reader who shares the author's frames of reference must be willing to bridge the semantic gap between the two terms. The impact of a metaphor depends on the width of that semantic gap. Georgian poetry seems so pretty and insipid to a modern reader (as it did to Hulme and the Imagists) because the gap was so narrow as to cause the juxtaposition to lack tension.

Collocability is of crucial importance to Hulme: he moves effortlessly from abstract to concrete and vice versa, In *Conversion* (see above, p. 127), the narrator "walked in the valley wood" to find that beauty stifled him "like a scented cloth/Cast over". In *As a Fowl*, the rays of the rising sun make the light look braided like a proud woman who has finished her toilet: "the tressed white light":

> As a fowl in the tall grass lies
> Beneath the terror of the hawk,
> The tressed white light crept
> Whispering with hand on mouth mysterious
> Hunting the leaping shadows in straight streets
> By the white houses of the old Flemish towns.

One of the two-line *Images* runs as follows:

> The lark crawls on the cloud
> Like a flea on a white body.

Richards' bipartition of metaphoric ingredients, viz. *tenor* (ie the idea or the subject) and *vehicle* (ie the image) will take us some way to a clearer understanding of Hulme's metaphors. One characteristic of them is that everyday objects are made the tenor (eg a mast, a tree, a man on the Embankment), and that, unlike many of his poetic predecessors, he does not take his vehicles from Classical Antiquity. Thus tenor and vehicle are 'on the same level', taken from our world and from the same conceptual realm. Another characteristic is that his metaphors are transitive. The exchange of meaning implied by a metaphor is often stated to be intransitive because the movement in one-directional, from the tenor, which is the focal point, towards the vehicle, which is peripheral except in one respect.

In our culture, we all understand the point of the metaphor ' Peter is a rat', and it would be peculiar for us to suggest that 'a rat is Peter'. However, the significant thing about Hulme's metaphors is that it is sometimes hard to tell which is the tenor and which the vehicle. Thus in the two-line *Image, Oh! Lady* a reader would be hard put to it to decide whether it is the love scene or the sea scene that is meant to be the tenor: is it a man making advances to a woman, or is it the description of the sea view that triggers off the erotic associations? In most cases, such sophistication does not confuse the reader or hamper his understanding – or enjoyment:

>   Oh, lady, to me full of mystery
>   Is that blue sea beyond your knee.

Most of Hulme's metaphors are bold, yet immediately intelligible; thus, transitions from day to night are compared to more or less successful theatrical performances. On the other hand, it would be wrong to pretend that his poetry always makes for effortless understanding. In *Susan Ann and Immortality* the sky is green and the clouds are brown like "chestnuts leaves arching the ground". However, nothing in the poem leads up to an autumn scene, and its relation with immortality remains obscure:

>   Her head hung down
>   Gazed at earth, fixedly keen,
>   As the rabbit at the stoat
>   Till the earth was sky,
>   Sky that was green,
>   And brown clouds past,
>   Like chestnut leaves arching the ground.

It is as if Hulme is sometimes carried away by his own creative vigour, which blurs the focus. In some cases he seems to be just playing with words and their sounds or idiosyncratic associations.

Synaesthesia – the device by which "one sensory experience is described in the vocabulary of another[10] occurs frequently. The technique harks back to Baudelaire's theory of *correspondances* and the Symbolists' efforts to bring poetry closer to music. Some of Hulme's most striking images are illustrations of synaesthesia. Usually sound and sight are involved. *The Embankment* talks about "the flash of gold heels on the pavement":

The Embankment
(the fantasia of a fallen gentleman on a cold, bitter night)

Once, in finesse of fiddles found I ecstasy,
In a flash of gold heels on the hard pavement.
Now see I
That warmth's the very stuff of poesy.
Oh, God, make small
The old star-eaten blanket of the sky,
That I may fold it round me and in comfort lie.

In the last lines of *Far back there* (cf. p. 130 above), the middle-aged princess "leans tranced in a dreamy curve/As a drowsy wail in an Eastern song".

Hulme creates a new world for his readers, or rather, a new perception of the world. To reach that goal he did not avail himself of an esoteric vocabulary, but mostly used the language that men use in everyday conversation. The sympathetic reader will agree to play Hulme's game, allow his world picture to be changed, and thus derive full benefit from the poems.

CHAPTER TWELVE

HULME CRITICISM

Michael Roberts' book from 1938, *T.E. Hulme*, is the first critical work devoted entirely to a treatment of Hulme's ideas. However, the main emphasis is on Hulme as a philosopher. Roberts is anxious to place him in the 'great' European tradition. His estimation of Hulme is coloured by his own Christian conviction, and it is as if he keeps many aspects of Hulme's thinking at arm's length. Hulme's aesthetic ideas are not given a very thorough-going analysis. Roberts is evidently not a literary expert, which makes his literary criticism lop-sided, not to say unfair.

Roberts makes scant use of quotation, there are hardly any work or page references, and it is often difficult to disentangle Hulme's thoughts from Roberts' – not infrequently negative – comments on them. About Hulme's poetry we are told that it contains "clear visual images" [1], but there is no analysis either of the images or of Hulme's poetry in a more general way. He justly criticizes Hulme for not attempting a definition of a successful image, and he points to the obvious paradox that Hulme claims that poetry should record particular sensations, but that he tends to indulge in descriptions of a universal kind in his poems[2].

Roberts does say that Hulme concentrates on one point within poetry, viz. technique[3]. But he does not mention the contemporary discussion of the impact of analogy, nor the heated debate about *vers libre*. He is vague on Hulme's conception of metaphor. All he says is that to Hulme the quality of a poem depends on the accuracy of observation[4], but he is not very informative with regard to Hulme's distinctive character as a poet.

Roberts is understandably critical of Hulme's simplification of the concept of Romanticism, which in Hulme's idiolect comes close to being synonymous with sentimentality[5]. He gives a cavalier treatment of Hulme's ideas of the imagination, "the act of apprehending things in their essence"[6], and he briefly refers to fancy as the instrument of expression of the imagination. But what we are given is a recapitulation rather than an analysis. The same objection can be raised to Roberts' discussion of two of Hulme's key terms, viz. counters and cinders. No attempt is made to look into the linguistic potentialities of those terms or Hulme's original use of them.

Of course Robert's book does give some idea of Hulme as a critic and as a poet, but the reader cannot help getting the impression that the book is a mild criticism of Hulme for not being more like the writer Roberts would have liked him to be.

Alun R. Jones' *The Life and Opinions of T.E.Hulme* (1960) is a traditional biography in the best sense of the word. The book consists of a mixture of data, quotations, summaries, and evaluations. The reader is given more biographical information than aesthetic criticism.

Jones recapitulates Hulme's essays carefully and loyally, giving his own assessment on the way. He points out the numerous discrepancies that are found in Hulme's aesthetic and philosophical thinking: thus, he is an anti-Romanticist, but at the same time an uncritical admirer of Bergson's mysticism. Jones characterizes Hulme's philosophical work as fragmentary, repetitive, and derivative (which is not entirely misleading) and sees his poetical theories as a function of his reading of Bergson.

Referring to Hulme's interest in the theory of poetry, Jones plausibly suggests that Hulme wrote his poems as illustrations of his own theories[7], and he pays tribute to Hulme for providing the theoretical framework within which young poets were able to conduct their experiments[8]. There is a brief reference to the question of a poet's relation to language, but Jones contents himself with saying that the image is the most important catalyst of the poetic synthesis. Hulme's poetry is given a summary treatment, without any examples[9].

The avowed intention of Jones' book is to separate facts from fictitious and popular ideas[10]. Jones obviously has an intimate knowledge of Hulme's works, and the book lives up to its title, covering most aspects of Hulme's thinking. Jones does not raise any forefingers, nor does he try to fit Hulme into a system or a category. Yet, despite its comprehensiveness, the book fails to do justice to Hulme's poems and to his achievement within aesthetic criticism. However, one great merit of Jones' book is that it prints Hulme's poems at the end, with a brief account of where they were first published and of Jones' own editorial procedure.

In 1936, Sir Herbert Read edited *T.E.Hulme, Speculations, Essays on Humanism and the Philosophy of Art.* The material of the book derives from published articles as well as unpublished notes. The foreword was written by Jacob Epstein, who says that he felt attracted by the vigour and sincerity of Hulme's thinking.

In his short biographical sketch, Read dwells on Hulme's military interests[11]. Within philosophy and aesthetics he was "by design" no systematic thinker – he was more of a poet, preferring to look at things "in the emotional light", and trying to grasp reality by means of metaphor rather than scientific analysis[12].

Read claims that Hulme had an ardent wish to write a book that was to deliver the ultimate proof that the world is not a whole, and that it is impossible to describe everything in words. However, all that remains are some fragments, collected by Read under the title of *Cinders*[13].

Read, who knew Hulme personally, has nothing to offer in the way of detailed analysis of, or comment on, Hulme' doctrines.

The introduction of Samuel Hynes' *Further Speculations* (1955) gives a short portrait of Hulme in which Hynes mentions the fact that Hulme's talk was reportedly full of images. Hynes calls Hulme a propagandist rather than a systematic thinker, labelling him the spokeman of avant-garde art in the service of a reactionary philosophy[14]. Hynes pertinently remarks that Hulme gave currency to thoughts that were not new, but which needed reformulation[15].

Hynes give Hulme credit for inspiring the counter-current leading away from 19th century Romanticism that set in during the first and second decades of the 20th century. But his treatment of Hulme's literary theories and practice is anything but profound: he touches sketchily on the problem of free verse, echoing a statement by Hulme to the effect that the purpose of Imagism was incompatible with the hypnotizing effect of regular metre[16]. Hynes does mention counters and cinders, but does not discuss Hulme's exploitation of the two terms. He is not impressed by Hulme's poems, pointing out, in a general way, that they contain quite a lot of what Hulme claims to be in oppostion to (generally speaking, Hynes considers Hulme very 'anti': anti-rationalist, anti-science, anti-Romanticist[17]), but he refrains from any analysis in the proper sense of the word.

The first-hand knowledge of Glenn Hughes enables him to give indispensable information about the data of Imagism and the members of the movement (*Imagism and the Imagists* (1931, repr. 1960)). Hughes has talked with several of the Imagists, and the theoretical part of his book testifies to his insight into, and his affection for, the theories and the theorists, including Hulme. He calls Hulme the father of Imagism, but he does not attempt any assessment of his doctrines, and among the Imagist poems he prints there is none by Hulme. In his presentation of the *vers libre* problem he does not go beyond the summarizing stage.

Stanley Coffman Jr (*Imagism, a Chapter for the History of Modern Poetry*, 1951) does not see Hulme merely as a function of somebody else, or his writings as a largely abortive attempt to establish a coherent and comprehensive theory. Coffman is virtually the only critic who considers Hulme's poems in their own right and not merely as sketchy illustrations of his literary theories. In Chapter Three of the book – *T.E.Hulme as Imagist* – we read that "Imagism *could* have its source in Hulme"[18]. Coffman subjects Hulme's doctrines to a careful analysis, making a comprehensive *explication de texte* of Hulme's essay *Classical and Romantic*, his *Lectures on Modern Poetry, Notes on Language and Style* and *Speculations*. Coffman gives a clear account of Hulme's indebtedness to Bergson[19], also as far as the writing of poetry is concerned.

Katherine Nott (*The Emperor's Clothes*, 1953) is mainly interested in Hulme as a philosopher, devoting a chapter (*Mr. Hulme's Sloppy Dregs*) to a searching analysis of original sin, and glancing on the way at his aesthetics. "Hulme's aesthetic theory, particularly when it is about the nature of poetry, is acute though limited"[20]. She blames Hulme for semantic sloppiness in his discussion of Classicism and Romanticism – the latter being identified by Hulme with "the man-centred humanism which he hates", and Classicism being seen as "the God-centred view of orthodox Christianity"[21].

Nott's own view, permeating the book, is that the scientific attitude is immediately applicable to also traditional humanist disciplines: "we therefore cannot say that there exist 'fields' in which The Scientist has nothing to tell us. *A fortiori* we cannot say that we can obtain another kind of 'knowledge' in those fields, by other methods"[22]. "The growing body of knowledge is unified…We know, if at all, in one way, not two"[23]. Accordingly, she blames Hulme for preserving "the whole content of 'Human Nature' for the field of nescience"[24]. Nott sees Hulme's purpose as that of combating mechanistic determinism and saving the doctrine of Free Will and the conception of unpredictability in the universe[25]. The title of her book is a clear indication of her lack of respect for Hulme and his theories.

Graham Hough's collection of essays, *Image and Experience. Studies in a Literary Revolution* (1960) is extremely critical of Imagism and the Imagists. Part One, *Imagism and its Consequences*, is a virulent attack on the way Eliot's predecessors chose to write poetry, and a concomitant defence of the good old English poetic tradition. Hough does not mince matters: the house of poetry has been uninhabitable since the days of Imagism[26]. He does not show any willingness to understand what the Imagists were getting at, and he blames Hulme for being the spokesman of "a depressed cosmic Toryism"[27] on the basis of the latter's essay *Classical and Romantic*. Hough does not outline a possible 'better' continuation of late Victorian poetry. His maxim is that poets ought to draw their material from people they know and address their writings to people they know[28], and he criticizes Hulme for falling short in both respects.

In *From Gautier to Eliot. The Influence of France on English Literature 1851-1939* (1960), Enid Starkie, the respected Romanist, gives competent information about the situation beyond the Channel. She sees the art for art's sake movement as a rebellion against Romanticism and moralizing art (which was also Hulme's point), but unfortunately she says very little about the theoretical considerations of Gustave Kahn. Starkie sees Hulme mainly as a disciple of Laforgue[29] and claims that he wanted to introduce *vers libre* in England[30]. She does not seem to be overwhelmingly impressed by Hulme's achievement.

C.K.Stead's *The New Poetic* (1964) analyses the shifts of emphasis that took place in the relations between poet, reader, and text, from late Victorianism to Eliot. Even though the avowed aim of the book is to look into "what conception of poetry is implied in the work of certain 20th century poets"[31], it says little about Hulme. Stead underlines Hulme's attack on the idea of the poet as a man of sentiment, a moralist, and a prophet, but the central figures of the book are Yeats and Eliot.

It is surprising to see how many aspects of Hulme's oeuvre are passed over in silence by his critics Most of them see a clear connection between Hulme and the Imagists, but though Imagism was given its name owing to its use of images, Stanley Coffman Jr, is the only critic who subjects Hulme's poetry to any kind of analysis. Most critics see Hulme's aesthetics as an inseparable part of his philosophy, which is justifiable, and they attack it for being incoherent and uncompromising, in some respects even disgusting.

In the light of Hulme's and his contemporaries' preoccupation with technical problems within poetry, such as free verse, it is remarkable that no critic should have commented on Gustave Kahn's pioneer treatise on *vers libre*. And the two key concepts in Hulme's linguistic thinking, viz. counters and cinders, pass virtually unnoticed by the great majority of his critics. No less strangely, the fact that Eliot's theory about the 'objective correlative' is clearly foreshadowed in Hulme's literary reflections is given only a passing reference.

Hulme does not rank very highly in the estimation of his critics: they are not very impressed by his achievements within poetry and aesthetics, and some of them find it hard to conceal their antipathy towards him as a man.

Conclusion

Positivism

Reality is one, and our method, viz. natural science, is the key to the understanding of it, said the Positivists. Down through the centuries, natural science has demonstrated the existence of truths, or laws, that have proved to be always valid, independent of time, country, or religion: the law of gravitation applies in all climates, and water is everywhere composed of oxygen plus hydrogen. Natural science is objective and transnational.

To the Positivists, reality was synonymous with the Greek *physis*, ie nature in the sense of 'that which is outside man'. Their main effort was directed towards finding new laws that would enhance our insight and teach us to read the book of nature with even greater understanding. At first, their investigations focussed on phenomena that were susceptible of mathematical, physical, and chemical analysis. But gradually their techniques were extended to other areas of knowledge, such as sociology. Characteristically, Herbert Spencer views philosophy in terms of biology.

The Positivists' conception of the world was a reductionist one. They did not discuss the extent or the limit of what they chose to call reality. They did not consider the possibility that the cognition furnished by natural science might be a human construct that did not necessarily have a corresponding 'reality' outside man, or, more generally, that the thing they called 'reality' may be a social construction. For surely, man-created phenomena like business and legislation are also aspects of 'reality'?

Add to this that the art of painting showed that *physis* can be viewed from several angles, and that D.W.Griffith's melodramatic films from the years 1908-1913 demonstrated a new temporal and spatial logic in the sequences. So, contrary to the Positivists' assumption, reality is *not* one.

And there was an 'inner reality' that the Positivists had largely ignored because they were suspicious of what could not be exactly measured or defined. Freud's introspective practice showed the existence of another world that had been outside the purview of Positivist analysis, which scorned 'subjectivity'. The same goes for the whole issue of personal and public morality.

The anti-Positivists, who became more articulate and influential especially after the turn of the century, felt uneasy about the closed circuit of Positivist thinking. What is at the root of their criticism is the realization that there is no position outside reason where you can lecture about reason and pass judgement on reason. Hence their refusal to give unquestioned priority to reason.

Imagism

Imagism is not a radical rupture with all its immediate and more distant predecessors. Virtually all the Imagist poets – and Hulme, too – were interested in, and inspired by, late 19th century French poetry, especially as far as the formal aspects were concerned. They also adopted the French convention of forming a 'school' – be it ever so loosely structured – and issuing a manifesto summing up what Imagism was, and containing some theoretical reflections. And the cult of the poetic image was not an Imagist invention – the metaphysical poets of the 17th century worked along the same lines. What singles the Imagists out is their belief that the image is not an ornamental device, but a shortcut to the true comprehension of reality.

Central to their thinking was the idea of dynamism. One source of inspiration could be Darwin's theory of evolution. In the first decade of the 20th century, dynamism is seen in the political fondness for drive and expansion that underlies imperialism and colonialism, in Freud's doctrine of urges, in William James' stream of consciousness theory, and in Bergson's hypotheses about the *élan*. So, politically, metaphysically, philosophically, and psychologically speaking, a basic tension is assumed between movement and stasis. The sophisticated thing about Hulme and the Imagists is that, in their poetry, they exploited the rhythm that arose from a juxtaposition of flux and poise.

Imagism rests on a speculative, almost metaphysical, basis, yet Imagist poetry shows a down-to-earth precision, which was undoubtedly a reaction against what was felt as the vagueness and fluidity of Impressionism and contemporary Georgian poetry. The discipline required particularly appealed to Hulme, witness his stance in religious and political matters.

Pound put a finger on the soft spot when, with considerable justification, he complained of the lack of an organic centre in an Imagist poem. Very often the poems, including Hulme's, have no paraphraseable meaning, partly because the poets devote all their energies to the play of contrasted or parallel images, and partly because the poems are open-ended, or stop seemingly unaccountably. But then again, the poets' intention was never to tell a story.

Hulme

Even if Hulme never called himself an Imagist, and never gained a position comparable to that of Pound among the Imagists, it is a fact that he was instrumental in fathering and propagating some of the ideas that came to be known as Imagist ones.

Bergson had maintained that the method of philosophy is the opposite of that of science. Hulme agreed, deploring the fact that philosophy had allowed itself to be lured into the precincts of science, for the inevitable consequence had been its downfall. As Hulme saw it, all philosophy of science must of necessity be untrue: representing the cosmos in words is as great a distortion as representing solidity in a plane of two dimensions[1]. Science owes its birth to someting essentially subjective and 'unscientific', he goes on to say. There exists no abstract or speculative system that does not have its origin in an act of intuition, or as the perception of a physical allegory[2].

It is true that Hulme's ideas were frequently borrowed ones, but the point is that they were not very well known in England. Like the Imagists, he was heavily indebted to French philosophy and literary theory. He said himself that the centre of interest had moved from Germany to France, which had led to increasing clarity[3]. He was fond of saying that art and art criticism between the Renaissance and his own day were of inferior quality. However, paradoxically, in his theory and practice he was profoundly influenced by French theories from the middle and the end of the 19th century.

Hulme thought that poetry should be the processed record of a significant glimpse[4]. He would have agreed with Valéry's statement that it is not our feelings but the pattern we make of them that is the centre of value. Hulme admits that the poet's observation of the surrounding world is something entirely subjective, which, however, does not make it less valid.

Considering his partiality for images and illustrative representation, it is surprising to see the scarcity of illuminating images and pithy exemplifications in his prose. His explanations, such as they are, not infrequently read like rationalizations after the fact, attempts to lend plausibility to the intuitively felt, purely subjective, constructs. In terms of linguistic originality and precision, Hulme's prose and poetry are poles apart.

The Legacy

It would be an exaggeration to call Hulme and the Imagists the originators of the wave of linguistic interest that dominated philosophy and literary criticism during most of the 20th century. But their achievement contributed to the rejuvenation of the word and to the systematic analysis of language and its function in literature, and the relationship between language and reality. Influential 20th century critics and 'schools' worked along the same lines and struggled with the same issues as Hulme and the Imagists.

T.S. Eliot

Eliot never met Hulme, but perhaps he read the latter's articles in *New Age*. At least he refers to Hulme's *Speculations*[5].

The two men shared some attitudes: they despised liberal humanism, and they were disillusioned with regard to human improvement. And, of course, they were both interested in poetry and the theory of poetry, and to some degree they drew on the same sources. Thus, it is perfectly imaginable that Eliot found Laforgue and other French poets and theorists via Hulme and the Imagists.

It is interesting to see the extent to which Eliot echoes or elaborates on some of Hulme's basic tenets: to Eliot, the goal towards which poets ought to aspire was "the firmness, the true coldness, of the genuine artist", and "poetry is not a turning loose of emotion, but an escape from emotion, it is not an expression of personality"[6]. The two men saw eye to eye over the principle of the objective correlative, and they were both averse to putting 'ideas' into poetry: a poem has being, not meaning. Consequently they were suspicious of moralization and didacticism in poetry.. The moral value of the poem resides in the accuracy of the image[7]. So Hulme's "exact model analogy" is, also morally speaking, an asset.

Eliot stands on the shoulders of Hulme rather than of the Imagists because Hulme was more preoccupied with theoretical issues than most of the Imagists were. What is in Hulme groping and tentative speculation becomes in Eliot a fully-fledged theoretical edifice.

In *Criterion II*, April 7, 1924 – ie several years after Hulme's death – Eliot calls Hulme the forerunner of a new attitude of mind, which ought to become the 20th century mind if the 20th century is to have a mind of its own. "Hulme is classical, reactionary, and revolutionary; he is the antipodes of the eclectic, tolerant, and democratic mind of the last century"[8].

LATER DEVELOPMENTS

The New Critics formed a 'school' like the Imagists, and, like them, they were preoccupied by the function of the word and the theory of poetry. They agreed with the Imagists and Hulme that poetry should not be didactic, and that the images should serve other purposes than merely decorative ones. They, too, wrote short poems and denied the existence of specific poetic words. However, to the New Critics, the strength of the poetic formulation resides in its ambiguity, which they called irony, and which is, of course, far removed from Hulme's 'hard and dry' verbal precision.

The Deconstructionists learned the technique of careful attention to language from the New Critics, and before them, from Hulme and the Imagists even though they are less concerned with what is conventionally regarded as the meaning of a word. In their interpretative practices they focus on what happens to the reader in the process, just as Hulme (and Eliot) did with their theory of the objective correlative.

The concept of reality was a challenge to the Deconstructionists as it was to Hulme and the Imagists. Both groups saw it in dynamic terms. To the Deconstructionists, reality is a series of 'present moments', each of them carrying reminiscences of the past and intimations of the future. Thus a rhythm arises between the 'now' and the 'not-now', analogous to Hulme's flux/stasis dichotomy.

FINAL REMARKS

Samuel Hynes gives a sweeping and rather cavalier treatment of Imagism and the Imagists: they were a short chapter in the history of English literature, provided with a name and a manifesto, and they have been taken more seriously than they deserve [9]. Even if the heyday of the movement was not a period that shook English poetry to its foundations, Hynes' value judgement is not quite fair, and it is obviously untrue.

What is reality? What are its characteristics? How can we describe it? Can we ever get to an understanding of it? Will our thinking capacity ever enable us to penetrate into "the deepest abysses of being" [10]? That aspiration was one of the driving forces behind Imagist practice. Hulme, too, felt that ancient longing to get closer to the *Ding and sich*, but his oeuvre seems to prove that he came to realize that it was an elusive concept and an unattainable goal.

But their untiring efforts are one reason why Hulme and the Imagists deserve to be taken seriously; another resason is the reorientation they heralded within the poetical and critical traditions. It is true that they were not initiators in all respects, but they were consciously working and very ingenious and committed bridge builders.

Bibliography

Abrams, M.H., *Doing Things with Texts. Criticism and Critical Theory.* New York & London 1989

Aiken, Conrad, 'The Place of Imagism'. *New Republic.* New York, May 22, 1915

Aiken, Conrad, *Scepticisms. Notes on Contemporary Poetry.* New York, Knopf 1919

Aldington, Richard, 'Modern Poetry and the Imagists'. *The Egoist,* June 1st 1914

Aldington, Richard, Assessment of F.S.Flint. *The Egoist,* June 1st 1914, and in the special Imagist number of *The Egoist*, May 1st 1915

Aldington, Richard, *Images 1910-1915.* The Poetry Bookshop, London 1915

Aldington, Richard, 'The Poetry of Ezra Pound'. The special Imagist number of *The Egoist*, May 1st 1915

Aldington, Richard, Assessment of the poetry of Amy Lowell. *The Egoist,* July 1st 1915

Aldington, Richard, *Literary Studies and Reviews.* London 1924

Aldington, Richard & Riding, Laura (eds.), *A Survey of Modernist Poetry.* London 1927

Aldington, Richard, selected and translated: *Rémy de Gourmont, Selections from All his Works.* 2 vols., Chicago, Covici 1928

Aldington, Richard, *The Complete Poems of Richard Aldington.* Allan Wingate. London 1929, 1948

Aldington, Richard, *Life for Life's Sake. A Book of Reminiscences.* London 1941

Allen, Don Cameron, *Image and Meaning: Metaphoric Traditions in Renaissance Poetry.* Baltimore 1960

Alquié, Ferdinand, *Philosophie du surréalisme.* Paris, Flammarion 1955

Alvarez, Alfred, *The New Poetry.* Penguin 1962

Aristotle's *Poetics,* tr. T. A. Moxou, Everyman's Library 901, Dent 1943

Arp, Hans, *On My Way: Poetry and Essays 1912-47.* New York 1948

Balakian, Anna, *Literary Origins of Surrealism.* University of London Press 1967

Balakian, Anna, *Surrealism, The Road to the Absolute.* Revised ed., Unwin Books 1972

Barthes, Roland, *Image Music Text* (transl. Stephen Heath). Fontana Press 1977

Bateson, F.W., *English Poetry: An Introduction.* London 1950

Beaunier, André, *La poésie nouvelle.* Paris 1901

Bergson, Henri, *Matière et Mémoire. Essai sur la relation du corps à l'esprit.* Paris 1900

Bergson, Henri, *L'évolution créatrice.* Paris 1908

Bergson, Henri, *Les deux sources de la morale et de la religion.* Paris 1932

Bigsby, C.W.E., *Dada et surréalisme.* London, Methuen 1972

Black, Max, *Models and Metaphors.* Cornell University Press 1962

Black, Max, *A Companion to Wittgenstein's Tractatus.* Cambridge University Press 1964

Blackmore, John, *Ernest Mach, a Deeper Look.* London 1992

Bodelsen, C.A., *T.S.Eliot's Four Quartets. A Commentary.* Copenhagen 1958

Braithwaite, William Stanley, 'Imagists and their Poetry'. Boston Transcript 21 April 1915

Braithwaite, William Stanley, 'Imagism: Another View'. *New Republic.* New York June 12 1915

Braithwaite, William Stanley, '*The Latest Quintessence of Imagism*'. Boston Transcript May 6 1916

Braunsvig, Marcel, *La littérature française contemporaine: 1850 à nos jours.* Paris, Colin 1926

Breton, André, *Qu'est-ce que le surréalisme?* Paris 1934. English translation by David Gascoigne, London Faber 1936

Breton, André, *Les manifestes du surréalisme.* Paris 1946

Brooke, Rupert, *The Letters of Rupert Brooke* (ed. Geoffrey Keynes). London, Faber 1968

Brooke-Rose, Christine, *A Grammar of Metaphor.* London 1965

Browder, Clifford, *André Breton; Arbiter of Surrealism.* Geneva, Librairie Droz 1967

Buckley, James H., *William Ernest Henley: A Study in the "Counter-Decadence" of the 'Nineties.* Princeton University Press 1945

Burdett, Osbert, *The Beardsley Period. An Essay in Perspective.* London 1925

Carter, Huntley, '*The New Rhythm*'. *The Egoist,* February 16 1914

Cassagne, A., *La théorie de l'art pour l'art en France chez les derniers romantiques et les premiers réalistes.* Paris, Hachette 1906

Cawes, Mary Ann, *Surrealism and the Literary Imagination (A Study of Breton and Bachelard)* The Hague/Paris, Mouton & Co 1966.

Cawes, Mary Ann, *The Poetry of Dada and Surrealism.* Princeton University Press 1970

Charlesworth, Barbara, *Dark Passages: The Decadent Consciousness in Victorian Literature.* University of Wisconsin Press 1965

Chesterton, G.K., *The Victorian Age in Literature.* London 1903
Cirlot, J.E., *A Dictionary of Symbols.* London 1962, 1983
Coffman, Stanley Jr., *Imagism, a Chapter for the History of Modern Poetry.* University of Oklahoma Press 1951
Comer, Cornelia A., '*Poetry Today*'. Atlantic Monthly, Boston April 1916
Comte, Auguste, *Cours de philosophie positive.* 6 vols, Paris 1830-1842
Comte, Auguste, *Système de politique positive.* Paris 1851-54
Comte, Auguste, *Pensées et préceptes* (ed. Georges Deherne). Paris 1924
Comte, Auguste, *Oeuvres choisies* (introd. Henri Gouhier). Paris 1943
Cornell, Ethel F., *The "Still Point".* New Brunswick Rutgers University Press 1962
Cornell, Kenneth, *The Post-Symbolist Period.* Yale University Press 1958
Cottle, Basil & Knights, L.C., (eds.), *Metaphor and Symbol.* London 1960
Cournos, John, '*Futurism*'. *The Egoist*, vol. IV, January 1917
Coutts-Smith, Kenneth, *Dada.* Studio Vista. London 1970
Cresson, André, *Hippolyte Taine, Sa Vie, Son Oeuvre.* Presses Universitaires de France 1951
Culler, Jonathan, *On Deconstruction. Theory and Criticism after Structuralism.* Routledge & Kegan Paul 1985
H.D., *Collected Poems.* London 1925
Daiches, David. '*T.E.Hulme and Eliot*' in *Poetry and the Modern World. A Study of Poetry in England between 1900 and 1939.* Chicago 1940
Daniells, E., '*T.S.Eliot and his Relation to T.E.Hulme*'. University of Toronto Quarterly II, April 1933
Danto, Arthur C., *The Transfiguration of the Commonplace.* Harvard University Press 1981
Davie, Donald, '*Syntax as Unpoetical. T.E.Hulme*' in *Articulate Energy: An Inquiry into the Syntax of English Poetry.* London 1955
Drinkwater, John, *Discovery. Being the Second Part of an Autobiography 1897-1913.* London 1932
Eastman, Max, *The Employment of Poetry.* New York 1913
Eco, Umberto, *The Role of the Reader.* Indiana University Press 1979
Ede, H.S., *Savage Messiah: A Life of Gaudier-Brzeska.* London 1931
The Egoist, An Individual Review, ed. Harriet S. Weaver. 1st issue, January 1, 1914. New York, Krans Reprint Corporation 1967
The Egoist, Special Imagist Number. May 1, 1915
Eliot, T.S., '*The Noh and the Image*'. *The Egoist*, vol. IV, August 1917
Eliot, T.S., '*Reflections on Contemporary Poetry*'. In two parts. *The Egoist,* September and November 1917
Eliot, T.S., *Selected Essays.* London, Faber & Faber 1932

Eliot, T.S., *The Use of Poetry and the Use of Criticism*. London, Faber & Faber 1933

Eliot, T.S. (ed.), *Literary Essays of Ezra Pound*. London 1954

Eluard, Paul, *Thorns of Thunder* (ed. George Reavey). Europe Press and Stanley Nott 1936

Elwin, Malcolm, *Old Gods Falling*. London 1939

Engell, James, *The Creative Imagination*. Harvard University Press 1981

Epstein, Jacob, *Epstein: An Autobiography*. New York 1955

Fairchild, Hoxie Neale, *'Hulme and the Imagists'* in *Religious Trends in English Poetry*, vol. V: *1880-1920: Gods of a Changing Poetry*. New York 1962

Farmer, Albert J., *Le mouvement esthétique et 'décadent' en Angleterre 1873-1900*. Paris 1931

Fenollosa, Ernest & Pound, Ezra, *'Noh' or Accomplishment. A Study of the Classical Stage of Japan*. London 1916

Fletcher, John Gould, *'Three Imagist Poets'. The Little Review*. New York, May 1916

Fletcher, John Gould, *Preludes and Symphonies*. A Combined edition of *Irradiations, Sand and Spray* and *Goblins and Pagodas*. Boston 1922. New edition 1930

Fletcher, John Gould, *'Ezra Pound'. A Review. Criterion,* London April 1929

Fletcher, John Gould, *Life Is My Song*. New York 1937

Flint, F.S., *In the Net of the Stars*. London, Elkin Matthews 1909

Flint, F.S., *'Contemporary French Poetry'. Poetry Review,* London 1912

Flint, F.S., *'Imagism'. Poetry.* Chicago, March 1913

Flint, F.S., poems printed in *The Egoist*, 1st January 1914

Flint, F.S., *'The History of Imagism'. The Egoist,* 1st May 1915

Flint, F.S., *'The Poetry of H.D.'.* The special Imagist number of *The Egoist,* 1st May 1915

Flint, F.S., *Envy. A Poem. The Egoist,* February 1917

Flint, F.S., *'Some French Poets of Today. A Commentary with Specimens'.* Monthly Chapbook London, October 1919

Flint. E.S., *Otherworld: Cadences*. London, Poetry Bookshop 1920

Flint, F.S., *'Verse Chronicle'. Criterion* XI, London July 1932

Flint. F.S., *'Biographical Sketch'* in *Collected Poems of Harold Monro*. London 1933

Fowlie, Wallace, *Climate of Violence: The French Literary Tradition from Baudelaire to the Present*. London, Secher & Warburg 1969

Le Gallienne, Richard, *English Poems* .4th edition, London & Boston 1895

Le Gallinenne, Richard, *The Romantic '90's*. New York, Putnam 1926

Gascoigne, David, *A Short History of Surrealism.* London, Cobden-Sanderson 1935. New Impression, London, Cass & Co. 1970
Gascoigne, David, *Man's Life, This Meat.* London, Parton Press 1936
Gaunt, William, *The Pre-Raphaelite Tragedy.* London 1942
Gaunt, William, *March of the Moderns.* London 1949
Gautier, Théophile, *Emaux et Camées.* Paris 1852
Gillie, Christopher, *Movemenets in English Literature 1900-1940.* Cambridge University Press 1975
Gourmont, Rémy de, *Le pèlerin du silence.* Orné d'un frontispice. Paris 1896
Gourmont, Rémy de, *Promenades philosophiques.* Paris. Société du Mercure de France, 1908
Gourmont, Rémy de, *Le livre des masques.* Paris 1911
Gourmont, Rémy de, *Le chemin de velours. Nouvelles dissociations d'idées.* Paris 1911
Gourmont, Rémy de, *Le problème du style.* Paris 1924
Gourmont, Rémy de, *Selections from all his Works.* Selected and translated by Richard Aldington. 2 vols. Chicago, Covici 1928
Grant, Joy, *Harold Monro and the Poetry Bookshop.* London, Routledge & Kegan Paul 1967
Graves, Robert, *Contemporary Techniques of Poetry. A Political Analogy.* The Hogarth Essays No. VIII. The Hogarth Press 1925
Graves, Robert, *Poetic Unreason and other Studies.* Cecil Palmer, 49, Chandos Street, 1925
Graves, Robert, *Good-Bye to All That. An Autobiography.* London 1929
Graves, Robert, *The Crowning Privilege.* London, Cassell 1955
Greensheet, Ferris, 'The Poetry of John Gould Fletcher'. The special Imagist number of *The Egoist* 1st May 1915
Hassall, Christopher, *Edward Marsh, Patron of the Arts.* London 1959
Hawkes, Terence, *Metaphor.* Methuen, The Critical Idiom Series, 1972
Henderson, Alice Corbin & Monroe, Harriet (eds.), *The New Poetry. An Anthology.* New York 1919
Henry, Leigh, *Mood Images. The Egoist,* 1st July 1916
Hibbard, Dominic, *The First World War. Context and Commentary.* London, Macmillan 1990
Hill, Archibald A., *Principles Governing Semantic Parallels.* Texas Studies in Literature and Language, 1. Austin, Texas 1959
Hough, Graham, *Image and Experience. Studies in a Literary Revolution.* London 1960
Howarth, Herbert, *Notes on Some Figures behind T.S.Eliot.* Boston 1964

Hughes, Glenn, *Imagism and the Imagists. A Study in Modern Poetry.* Stanford University Press 1931. Repr. 1960

Hulme, T.E., A translation of Bergson's *Introduction to Metaphysics.* London 1913

Hulme, T.E., '*Notes on Language and Style*' (ed. Herbert Read). Criterion III, July 1925

Hynes, Samuel (ed.), *Further Speculations of T.E.Hulme.* University of Minnesota Press 1955

Hynes, Samuel, *Edwardian Occasions: Essays on English Writing in the Early Twentieth Century.* London 1972

Hynes, Samuel, *A War Imagined.* London 1990

Imagist Anthology 1930 (foreword by Glenn Hughes), New York, Krans Reprint Co. 1970

Some Imagist Poets. Boston & London 1916, 1917

Isaacs, J., *The Background of Modern Poetry.* London 1951

Jackson, Holbrook, *The Eighteen Nineties. A Review of Art and Ideas at the Close of the Nineteenth Century.* New York 1927

Jakobson, Roman, '*The Metaphoric and Metonymic Poles*' in Jakobson, Roman & Halle, M., *Fundamentals of Language.* Janus Linguarum, Mouton 1953

Jepson, Edgar, *Memories of an Edwardian and Georgian.* London 1937

Johnson, Mark & Lakoff, George; *Metaphors We Live By.* University of Chicago Press 1980

Jones, Alun R., *The Life and Opinions of T.E.Hulme.* Beacon Press, Boston 1960

Kahn, Gustave, *Premiers poèmes précédés d'une étude sur le vers libre.* Paris 1897

Kahn, Gustave, *Le vers libre.* Paris 1912

Katz, J., *Semantic Theory.* New York 1972

Kenner, Hugh, *The Poetry of Ezra Pound.* London 1951

Kenner, Hugh, *The Pound Era.* University of California Press 1971

Kermode, Frank, '*T.E.Hulme*' in *Romantic Image.* London 1957

Kittay, E., *Metaphor, Its Cognitive Force and Linguistic Structure.* Oxford University Press 1987

Knights, L.C. & Cottle, Basil (eds.). *Metaphor and Symbol.* London 1960

Krieger, Murray, '*The Ambiguous Anti-Romanticism of T.E.Hulme*'. ELH 20, 1953

Krieger, Murray, *The New Apologists.* London 1956

Laforgue, Jules, *Oeuvres complètes. Mélanges posthumes.* Paris 1903

Lakoff, George & Turner, Mark, *More than Cool Reason: A Field Guide to Poetic Metaphor.* University of Chicago Press 1989

Lalou, René, *Histoire de la littérature française contemporaine.* Paris 1924

Leavis, F.R., *New Bearings in English Poetry.* Chatto & Windus 1932. Penguin 1963

Lehmann, John, *A Nest of Tigers: Edith, Osbert and Sacheverell Sitwell in their Times.* London 1968

Lehmann, John, *The English Poets of the First World War.* London 1981

Lemaître, Georges, *From Cubism to Surrealism.* Cambridge, Mass. 1945

Lemaître, Jules, *Les contemporains.* 8 vols., Paris 1886 et seq.

Lentricchia, Frank, *After the New Critics.* University of Chicago Press 1980

Lester, John A. Jr., *Journey through Despair 1880-1914: Transformations in British Literary Culture.* Princeton University Press 1968

Lewis, Wyndham, 'The Cubist Room'. *The Egoist*, 1st January 1914

Lewis, Wyndham (ed.), *Blast, Review of the Great English Vortex.* Numbers 1-2, 1914-1915, New York, Krans Reprint Corporation 1967

Lewis, Wyndham, *The Art of Being Ruled.* London Chatto & Windus 1926

Lewis, Wyndham, *Blasting and Bombardiering.* London 1937

Levin, Samuel R., *The Semantics of Metaphor.* Johns Hopkins University Press 1977

The Little Review, eds. Margaret Anderson, Jane Heap, Ezra Pound, John Rodker *et alii.* New York, 1914-1929

Lipps, Theodor, *Raumästetik und geometrisch-optische Täuschungen.* Heidelberg 1897

Lipps, Theodor, *Die etischen Grundfragen.* Heidelberg 1905

Lipps, Theodor, *Grundlegung der Ästetik.* Vols. 1-2. Hamburg & Leipzig 1903-1906

Lipps, Theodor, *Naturwissenschaft und Weltanschauung.* Heidelberg 1906

Lipps, Theodor, *Philosophie und Wirklichkeit.* Heidelberg 1908

Lowell, Amy, *A Dome of Many-Coloured Glass.* Boston 1912

Lowell, Amy, *Sword Blades and Poppy Seed.* Oxford 1914

Lowell, Amy, several poems printed in *The Egoist* February 16, 1914

Lowell, Amy, 'A Letter from London'. *Little Review* I, September 1914

Lowell, Amy, some poems printed in *The Egoist* July 1st 1915

Lowell, Amy, an assessment of her poetry by Richard Aldington. *The Egoist* July 1st 1915

Lowell, Amy, *Six French Poets. Studies in Contemporary Literature.* New York 1915

Lowell, Amy, *Tendencies in Modern American Poetry.* Boston & New York 1917

Lowell, Amy, several poems printed in Harriet Monroe & Alice Corbin Henderson (eds.) *The New Poetry. An Anthology.* New York 1919

Lowell, Amy, '*Amy Lowell and the Art of Poetry*' by Archibald Macleish in *North American Review.* New York, March 1925

Lowes, John Livingstone, '*An Unacknowledged Imagist*'. *Nation,* New York, February 24, 1916

Lowes, John Livingstone, *Selected Poems of Amy Lowell.* Boston 1928

Lüdi, Georges, *Die Metapher als Funktion der Aktualisierung.* Collection Romanica Helvetica vol. 85. Bern 1973

Mach, Ernest, *Die Analyse der Empfindungen.* Leipzig 1886

Mach, Ernest, *Die Leitgedanken meiner naturwissenschaftlichen Erkenntnislehre und ihre Aufnahme durch die Zeitgenossen. Sinnliche Elemente und naturwissenschaftliche Begriffe.* Leipzig 1919

Maintenant (ed. Arthur Cravan); 5 issues, Paris 1912-1915

Maitre, Doreen, *Literature and Possible Worlds.* Pembridge Pres ltd 1983

Marsh, Edward, *A Number of People.* London 1939

Martin, Marianne W., *Futurist Art and Theory 1909-15.* Oxford, Clarendon Press 1968

Martin, Wallace, *The New Age under Orage: Chapters in English Cultural History.* Manchester University Press 1967

Matthiessen, F.O., *The Achievement of T.S.Eliot.* Oxford University Press 1947

Michaud, Guy, *Message poétique du symbolisme.* Vols 1-3, Paris 1947

Michel, Walter & Fox, C.V. (eds.), *Wyndham Lewis on Art (Collected Writings 1913-56).* London, Thames & Hudson 1969

Mill, John Stuart, *Auguste Comte and Positivism.* London 1865. Ann Arbor Paperback 1961

Mill, John Stuart, *A System of Logic.* London 1843

Mill, John Stuart, *Utilitarianism.* London 1861

Mill, John Stuart, *The Subjection of Women.* London 1869

von Mises, Richard, *Ernst Mach und die empirische Wissenschaftsauffassung.* 's-Gravenhage 1938

Monro, Harold, '*Imagism and Imagists*'. *The Egoist* May 1st 1914

Monro, Harold, '*The Imagists discussed*'. The special Imagist number of *The Egoist,* May 1st 1915

Monro, Harold, *Collected Poems.* With a biographical sketch by F.S. Flint. London 1933

Monroe, Harriet (ed.), *Poetry: A Magazine of Verse.* New York 1912-13

Monroe, Harriet & Henderson, Alice Corbin (eds.), *The New Poetry. An Anthology.* New York 1919

Murray, John Middleton, *The Problem of Style.* Oxford University Press 1925

Nelson, Francis W., *Valet to the Absolute: A Study of the Philosophy of T.E.Hulme.* University of Wichita Bulletin No. 22, 1950

Nordmann, Jean-Thomas, *Taine et la critique scientifique.* Presses Universitaires de France 1992
Norman, Charles, *Ezra Pound.* New York 1960. Revised ed, 1969
Nott, Kathleen, *The Emperor's Clothes.* London 1953
Nowottny, Winifred, *The Language Poets Use.* London 1965
O'Connor, William Van, *An Age of Criticism 1900-1950.* Chicago 1952
O'Keefe, Paul, *Gaudier-Brzeska: an Absolute Case of Genius.* Allan Lane 2003
Olsen, Flemming, *Elements of Textual Analysis.* Gyldendal, Copenhagen 1986
Ortony, Andrew (ed), *Metaphor and Thought.* Cambridge University Press 1979
Ortony, Andrew, '*Aspects of Metaphor*' in Honeck, R. & Hoffman, R. (eds.), *Cognition and Figurative Language.* Hillsdale, N.Y.: Laurence Erlbaum, Hillsdale 1980
Paige, D.D.(ed.), *The Letters of Ezra Pound 1907-40.* New York 1950. London 1951
Parfitt, George, *English Poetry of the First World War: Contexts and Themes.* London Harvester-Wheatsheaf 1990
Pater, Walter, *Selected Works* (ed. Richard Aldington). London 1948
Peckham, Morse, *Beyond the Tragic Vision.* London 1962
Pinto, Vivian de Sola, *Crisis in English Poetry 1880-1940.* Hutchinson University Library 1951, 1965
Pound, Ezra, '*A Few Don'ts by an Imagist*' in *Poetry,* Chicago, March 1913
Pound, Ezra, *Canzoni & Ripostes.* London 1913
Pound, Ezra, '*The New Sculpture*'. *The Egoist,* 16 February 1914
Pound, Ezra & Fenollosa, Ernest, '*Noh' or Accomplishment: A Study of the Classical Stage of Japan.* London 1916
Pound, Ezra, '*Vers libre and Arnold Dolmetsch*'. *The Egoist* , vol. IV, July 1917
Pound, Ezra, *Umbria:* the early poems of Ezra Pound, all that he now wishes to keep in Circulation from *Personae, Exultations, Ripostes,* etx. With translations from Guida Cavalcanti and Arnaut Daniel and poems by the late T. E.H. London, E. Matthews 1920
Pound, Ezra, *Personae. The Collected Poems of Ezra Pound.* New York 1926
'*Ezra Pound*'. A review by John Gould Fletcher. *Criterion,* London, April 1929
Pound, Ezra, *Make It New. Essays by Ezra Pound.* London 1934
Pound, Ezra, *Polite Essays.* London 1937
Pound, Ezra, *Gaudier-Brzeska. A Memoir.* The Marvell Press 1960
Pound, Ezra, *Letters to James Joyce.* London, Faber 1968
Pulos, C.E., '*T.E.Hulme*' in *The New Critics and the Language of Poetry.* University of Nebraska Studies, New Series, No. 19. Lincoln, Nebraska 1958
Quenell, Peter, *John Ruskin.* Longman 1956

Ray, Paul C., *The Surrealist Movement in England.* Cornell University Press 1971
Raymond, Marcel, *De Baudelaire au surréalisme.* R.A.Corréa, Paris 1933
Read, Forrest. *'76 (Seventy-Six), One World, and the Cantos of Ezra Pound.* Chapel Hill 1981
Read, Sir Herbert (ed.), *Speculations: Essays on Humanism and the Philosophy of Art.* London 1924
Read, Sir Herbert, *Reason and Romanticism.* Faber & Gwyer, London 1926
Read Sir Herbert, *Poetry and Anarchism.* London, Faber 1938
Read, Sir Herbert, 'The Isolation of the Image. T.E.Hulme' in *The True Voice of Feeling. Studies in English Romantic Poetry.* London 1952
Ribot, Théodule, *Essai sur l'imagination créatrice.* Paris 1900
Richards, I.A., *The Philosophy of Rhetoric.* Oxford University Press 1936
Richter, Hans, *Dada, Art and Anti-Art.* Translated from the German by David Britt. Thames & Hudson, London 1965
Rickword, Edgell, *Rimbaud, the Boy and the Poet* . Heinemann, London 1924
Riding, Laura & Aldington, Richard (eds.), *A Survey of Modernist Poetry.* London 1927
Riding, Laura, '*T.E.Hulme, the New Barbarism, and Gertrude Stein*' in *Contemporaries And Snobs.* New York 1928
Roberts, Michael, *T.E.Hulme.* London 1938
Rogers, Robert, *Metaphor: A Psychoanalytic View.* Berkeley 1978
Rogers, Timothy (ed.), *Georgian Poetry 1911-1922.* The Critical Heritage, London, Routledge 1977
Rorty, Richard, *Philosophy and the Mirror of Nature.* Princeton University Press 1979
Ross, Robert H., *The Georgian Revolt. Rise and Fall of a Poetic Ideal 1910-22.* London, Faber 1967
Ruskin, John, *Sesame and Lilies.* London 1871
Ruskin, John, *Lectures on Art.* London 1906
Ruthven, K. K., *The Conceit.* Methuen, The Critical Idiom Series. 1969
Ruthven, K.K., *Critical Assumptions.* Cambridge University Press 1979
Ruthven, K.K., *Ezra Pound as a Literary Critic.* Critics of the Twentieth Century. Routledge & Kegan Paul 1990
Scarfe, Francis, *Auden and After: The Liberation of Poetry 1930-41.* Routledge & Kegan Paul 1942
Schuchard, Ronald, '*Eliot and Hulme in 1916: Toward a Revaluation of Eliot's Critical and Spiritual Development*'. PMLA 88, 1973
Scott-James, Rolfe A., *Fifty Years of English Literature 1900-50.* London 1951
Scruton, Roger, *Art and Imagination.* Methuen 1974

Searle, J.R., '*Metaphor*' in Ortony, A. (ed.), *Metaphor and Thought*. Cambridge University Press 1979

Shapiro, Karl, '*T.S.Eliot. The Death of Literary Judgement*' in *In Defence of Ignorance* New York 1960

Shattuck, Roger, *The Banquet Years. The Origins of the Avant-Garde in France: 1885 to World War I*. London, Cape, revised ed. 1969

Sinclair, May, '*The Poems of Richard Aldington*'. *The English Reviewer* London, May 1921

Sinclair, May '*The Poems of H.D.*' *Dial*. New York, February 1922

Sitwell, Edith, *The Wooden Pegasus*. Oxford 1920

Sitwell, Edith, *A Poet's Notebook*. London 1944

Sitwell, Edith, *Selected Letters* (eds. Lehmann & Parker) London 1970

Sitwell, Edith, *Taken Care of. An Autobiography*. London 1965

Sorel, Georges, *Réflexions sur la violence*. Paris 1906

Sorel, Georges, *Les illusions du progrès*. Paris 1908

Sorel, Georges, *Matériaux d'une théorie du prolétariat*. 1914. Published, Paris 1918

Sorel, Georges, *De l'utilité du pragmatisme*. Paris 1917

Spencer, Herbert, *The Principles of Psychology*. London 1855

Spencer, Herbert, *On Education*. London 1861

Spencer, Herbert, *A System of Synthetic Philosophy*. Ten vols., London 1862-93

Spencer, Herbert, *The Study of Sociology*. 2nd ed., London 1874

Spencer, Herbert, *The Man versus the State*. London 1884

Spencer, Herbert, *First Principles*. 5th impr., London 1915

Stansky, Peter, *On or About December 1910: Early Bloomsbury and its Intimate World*. Harvard University Press 1996,1997

Starkie, Enid, *From Gautier to Eliot: The Influence of France on English Literature 1851-1939*. London, Hutchinson 1960

Stead, C.K., *The New Poetic: Yeats to Eliot*. London, Hutchinson 1964

Sturrock, John (ed.), *Structuralism and Since. From Lévi-Strauss to Derrida*. Oxford University Press 1979

Swinnerton, Frank, *The Georgian Literary Scene 1910-35. A Panorama*. London 1950

Swinnerton, Frank, *Background with Chorus*. London 1956

Symons, A.J.A., *An Anthology of 'Nineties' Verse with an Introduction*. Matthews & Marriot 1928

Symons, Arthur, *The Symbolist Movement in Literature*. London 1899

Symons, Arthur, *Poems*. 2 vols. London, Heinemann 1901

Taine, Hippolyte, *Philosophie de l'Art*. Corpus des oeuvres de philosophie en langue française. Texte revu par Stéphane Douailler. Fayard 1985

Tate, Allen, '*Poetry and the Absolute*'. Sewanee Review XXXV, January 1927

Taupin, René, *L'influence du symbolisme français sur la poésie américaine (de 1910 à 1920)*. Paris 1929

Thompson, Silvanus, *The Life of William Thomson, Baron Kelvin of Largs*. Vols 1-2. London, Macmillan 1910

Thomsen, Chresten Kold, '*Reader-Response Criticism as Ideological Criticism*' in *Traditions and Innovations*. Papers presented to Andreas Haarder. Pre-Publications of the English Department of Odense University. Special Issue, June 1994

Tindall, William York, *Forces in Modern British Literature 1885-1956*. New York 1956

Trotter, David, *The Making of the Reader: Language and Subjectivity in Modern American, English, and Irish Poetry*. London 1984

Turner Mark & Lakoff, George, *More than Cool Reason: A Field Guide to Poetic Metaphor*. University of Chicago Press 1989

Turquet-Milnes, G., *The Influence of Baudelaire in France and England*. London 1913

The Tyro (ed. Wyndham, Lewis), Nos. 1-2, London 1921-22

Untermeier, Louis, *The New Era in American Poetry*. New York 1919

Untermeier, Louis, *American Poetry since 1900*. New York, Holt 1923

Untermeier, Louis, *Modern British Poetry*. New York 1920

Untermeier, Louis, *Modern American Poetry. A Critical Anthology*. New York 1942

Wees, William C., *Vorticism and the English Avant-Garde*. Manchester University Press 1972

Wheels. An Anthology of Verse (ed. Edith Sitwell). Six issues (Cycles 1-6), 1916-22

Wilde, Oscar, *Poems*. David Boyne 1881

Wilkinson, Marguerite, *New Voices. An Introduction to Contemporary Poetry*. New York 1919

Williams, Raymond, '*T.E.Hulme*'. In *Culture and Society 1780-1850*. London 1958

Williamson, George, *A Reader's Guide to T.S.Eliot. A Poem by Poem Analysis*. New York, Noonday Press 1957

Wilson, Edmund, *Axel's Castle. A Study in the Imaginative Literature of 1879-1930*. New York 1931

Wingfield-Stratford, Esmé, *Victorian Tragedy*. London 1930

Wingfield-Stratford, Esmé, *The Victorian Sunset*. London 1932

Wingfield-Stratford, Esmé, *Victorian Aftermath*. London 1934

Wittgenstein, Ludwig, *Tractatus logico-philosophicus*. Vienna 1922

Wittgenstein, Ludwig, *Philosophische Untersuchungen/Philosophical Investigations.* Cambridge University Press 1953

Worringer, Wilhelm, *Abstraktion und Einfühlung* (1907). Translated by Michael Bullock, *Abstraction and Empathy. A Contribution to the Psychology of Style.* New York 1967

Worringer, Wilhelm, *Formprobleme der Gotik* (1912). Translated by Sir Herbert Read, *Form Problems of the Gothic.* London 1927

Young, Alan, *Dada and After. Extremist Modernism and English Literature.* Manchester University Press 1981

Alphabetical Index

absolutes 45, 83-84, 88, 89, 97, 100, 106
abstraction 15, 21, 29, 42, 54, 72, 73, 80, 83, 93, 96, 118
action 70, 71
aesthetics 34, 49, 50, 51, 63, 72, 78, 81, 91, 93, 96, 97, 98, 137, 138, 140, 141
Aldington 11, 13, 16, 19, 55, 76, 77
alexandrine 74
analogy 14, 20, 34, 54, 68, 72, 88, 91, 97, 102, 103, 104, 106, 112, 113, 115, 117, 118, 137 145
architecture 51, 52, 99
argumentation 82-83, 91, 99
Aristotle 12, 14, 16, 100, 102, 114
Arnold, Matthew 53, 103
art for art's sake/ *l'art pour l'art* 49, 50-51, 58, 140
Austin 16
avant-garde 139

Bacon 31
Barthes, Roland 121
Baudelaire 17, 49, 50, 51, 52, 53, 54, 103, 134
Baumgarten 50, 53
Beardsley 13
beauty 15, 40, 57, 58, 79, 92, 94, 95, 96-97, 101, 107, 108, 116
the beholder 15, 86, 96, 98, 116, 131
Bergson, 24, 39, 52, 69-72, 74, 76, 81, 85, 86, 87, 89, 91, 97, 100, 115, 118, 138, 140, 144
biology 25, 27, 29, 34, 35, 36, 38, 39, 42, 69, 74, 82, 94, 98, 109, 132, 143, 145
Blach, Max 133
BLAST 21
Bohr, 15, 62
Brooke, Rupert 81
Byron 96

cadence 20, 77, 78
Canzoni and Ripostes 11
Carlyle 64
Carter, Huntley 76
categorization 68-69. 83, 87, 88, 98, 116, 117, 123
Cézanne 20, 51, 72, 95
cinders 79, 107, 113-116. 118, 127, 137, 139, 141
classical and romantic 95-96, 98, 106, 140
cliché 114
Coleridge 56, 92, 96, 104, 106, 112
comparison 75, 114
Comte 30-33, 37, 38, 39, 40, 41, 42, 43, 44, 45, 46, 68
conrete 93
connotation 113
content 15, 74, 75, 77, 78, 83, 91, 93, 108, 111, 112
Copernicus 98
correspondences/ *correspondances* 17, 49, 50, 57, 64, 74, 131
counters 103, 105, 112, 113-116, 127, 137, 139, 141
creation 18, 35, 36, 45, 46, 47, 54-55, 61, 63, 73, 89, 96, 97, 98, 100, 102, 103-106, 117
Croce 89
Criterion II 145
Cubism 63, 82, 92, 94
Mme Curie 68

dance 78-80, 115
Dante 40, 110
Darwin 28, 34, 38, 39, 45, 87, 109, 144
Debussy 63
Deconstructionism 20, 56, 88, 105, 147
deduction 24, 26, 31, 33, 34, 36, 38, 43, 46
Derrida 85, 120
denotation 15, 16, 113, 115
Descartes 31
Des Imagistes 12
determinism 14, 36, 38, 40, 49, 84, 87, 140
development 15, 28, 30, 34, 38, 39, 41, 69, 78, 88, 89, 94, 98, 101, 129
Dewey 25
dichotomy 32, 70, 85, 93, 103, 108, 111, 147
didacticism 50, 92, 95, 97, 101, 103, 114, 119, 124, 145, 147

durée 70-71
dynamism 21, 28, 29, 38, 39, 44, 45, 58, 67, 68-69, 74, 75, 76, 78, 89, 117, 144, 147

ecstasy 88, 102, 104, 130
the Edwardian Age 13, 91, 108
The Egoist 11, 12, 13, 16, 19, 20, 55, 77
Egyptian art 58, 73, 94
Einstein 28, 62, 63, 131
élan 24, 69-70, 87, 89, 144
Eliot 9, 20, 21, 58, 73, 77, 78, 119, 120, 140, 141, 145, 147
empathy 69
epiphany 70, 88, 102, 106
Epstein 63, 72, 94, 99, 138
eroticism 56, 78, 125, 130, 132
evolution 28, 29 30, 38, 43, 85, 87, 88, 89, 98, 144

fancy 56, 81, 92, 106, 137
finality 70
Flaubert, 16
Fletcher 19, 50, 78, 108
Flint 11, 12, 16, 71, 77, 78, 108
flux 38, 39, 70, 73, 85, 86, 89, 94, 96, 100, 101, 144, 147
Ford 101
form 15, 16, 20, 21, 29, 51, 53, 54, 56, 57, 59, 63, 68, 72, 74, 76, 77, 78, 91, 93, 94, 96, 104, 105, 108-110, 114, 115, 116, 118, 128-129, 144
form versus content 108, 111
formula 44
free verse, see *vers libre*
Freud 63, 68, 126, 143, 144
Fry, Roger 13
Futurism 82

Galilei 31
Gaudier-Brzeska 12, 51, 63, 69, 94, 99, 101, 118
Gautier 16, 54, 75
general/generalization 14, 26, 29 31, 32, 34, 35, 38, 40, 61, 80, 97, 98, 115
geometrical art 21, 51, 56, 63, 72, 73, 83, 93-95, 99
Georgian poetry 13, 91, 108, 133, 144
God 62, 68, 70, 83, 95, 115, 131, 140

Goncourt 50
Gourmont 55-57, 75, 78
Griffith, D.W. 143

hard and dry 84, 94, 99, 100, 106, 114, 115, 123, 147
H.D. 12, 20
Hegel 44
Heraclitus 61, 68
Homer 91
Horace 91, 105
humanism 87-88
Hume, David 67, 68

idea 89, 90, 91, 98, 105, 112, 145
ideal 90, 97, 98, 101, 111, 114, 120
ideogram 19
image 15, 16, 17, 18, 19, 34, 40, 54, 55, 56, 57, 58, 64, 65, 67, 70, 72, 85, 88, 89, 91 97-98, 100, 101, 102, 103, 105, 109, 110, 111, 112, 113, 114, 115, 116, 117, 119, 120, 125, 127, 128, 132-135, 137, 138, 144, 145
imagery 40, 55, 57, 58, 65, 108, 132
Imagist Anthologies 16, 17, 19, 20, 76
imagination 31, 38, 40, 41, 42, 43, 47, 55, 56, 63, 81, 92, 102, 106, 117, 137
imitation 14, 52, 54, 72, 73, 82, 110
Impressionism 16, 109, 144
induction 31, 35, 36, 38
infinity 88, 116
intellect 18, 19, 33, 34, 49, 61, 69, 85-86, 87, 93, 105
intensity 15, 79
intention 104, 109
intuition 40, 69, 70, 72, 83, 85-86, 89, 91, 93, 112, 132
invention 104

James,.William 68, 86, 144
Dr. Johnson 56

Kahn, Gustave 53, 59, 74-75, 77, 109, 140, 141
Kant 25, 79, 96
Keats 46, 96
Kelvin 23-24, 25, 42

Laforgue 53, 57-59, 74, 140, 145
Lamartine 96
landscape 35, 57, 125
Lemaître 65
Lenin 63
Lessing 127
Lewis, Wyndham 12, 16, 20
Lipps, Theodor 49, 51-52, 74, 89
Locke 55
Longinus 15
Lowell, Amy 12, 17, 19, 20, 77

Mach, Ernst 27-28, 38, 40, 41, 42
Mallarmé 63
manifolds 86-87, 92, 93, 97
Marsh 79
Marx 89
matter 27, 28, 29 42, 43, 44, 69, 70, 71, 87, 115
Maurras 98
mechanism 29, 41, 46, 69, 86, 87, 89, 100, 109, 140
metaphor 34, 49, 51, 55, 56, 58, 62, 75, 85, 89, 95, 104, 106, 111, 113, 114, 115, 117, 132, 137, 138
metaphysical poets 109, 144
metaphysics 28, 41, 51, 69, 84
metre 17, 57, 58, 68, 76, 78, 108, 109, 110, 111
Millet 107
Milton 107, 110
mimesis 14, 18, 19, 53-54, 56, 92, 101, 107-108
Monet 63, 96
Monro, Harold 13, 17, 18, 20
Monroe, Harriet 12
morals 31, 32, 33, 34, 46, 50, 52, 54, 64, 74, 81, 85, 97, 140, 141, 143, 145
Moréas 64
motion 29, 33, 41, 43, 44, 68, 69, 70, 73, 77, 92, 132, 144

narration 56, 57, 58, 116, 124
nature 23, 25, 27, 29, 35, 36, 50, 62, 72, 73, 84, 92, 94, 108, 111, 116, 126, 143
Neo-Classicism 17, 18, 36, 91, 95
Nerval 37

New Age 12, 13, 61, 81, 145
New Criticism 147
New Freeman 19
Newton 23, 62
Nietzsche 16, 37
Noh 19, 78

objective correlative 73, 118-121, 124, 141, 145, 147
observation 14, 15, 24, 25, 27, 32, 35, 37, 38, 40, 43, 61, 62, 67, 84, 106, 124, 127, 131, 137, 145
Orage 13
Original Sin 81, 83, 84, 87, 89, 95, 98, 140
Ostwald, Wilhelm 27

Parnassiens 64, 109
Pascal 41, 84
Pater 53
Peirce 43
perception 71, 135, 145
personification 57
phrase 112
physics 22, 28. 29, 30, 32, 41, 42, 61, 62, 70, 125, 143
Picasso 63, 94
Planck 61
Plato 54, 91, 96, 108
Poe 50, 64
poetic diction 15, 18, 75, 116, 130
Poetry: A Magazine of Verse 12, 17
The Poetry Review 13, 108
Poincaré 61
poise 89, 100 101, 105, 144
politics 32, 81, 83, 98, 144
Pope 78, 109, 111
Pound 11, 14, 16, 18, 19, 21, 62, 77, 79, 91, 98, 118, 144, 145
Pre-Raphaelites 50
progress 39, 46, 83, 85, 88, 89, 98
Proust 33, 131
psychology 25, 27, 29, 32, 35, 40, 51, 55, 68, 69, 102, 105, 108, 114

the reader 14, 15, 16, 18, 19, 45, 55, 58, 64, 65, 70, 72, 73, 81, 86, 96, 101, 110, 113, 114, 115, 117, 119, 120, 121, 124, 129, 131, 133

reality 14, 15, 16, 20, 23, 25-26, 32, 37, 38, 41, 42, 43, 44, 45, 49, 50, 52, 53, 54, 56, 57, 61 62, 64, 67, 68, 70, 72, 86, 92, 96, 98, 100, 101, 107, 116, 117, 125, 131, 138, 143, 144, 145, 147

the recipient 72, 92, 117, 120

religion 25, 32, 35, 37, 45, 46, 62, 81, 83, 84, 87-88, 95, 98, 99, 100, 105, 115, 126, 144

Renaissance 13, 39, 52, 58, 72, 82, 84, 94, 100, 145

representation 18, 68, 71, 92, 117

rhetoric 102, 129

rhyme 12, 56, 59, 75, 78, 129

rhythm 17, 18, 59, 68, 71, 74, 75, 76, 77, 78, 99, 101, 110, 118, 128, 144, 147

Ribot, Théodule 54-55, 74, 117

Richards, I.A. 111, 133

Rimbaud 53, 57

Rodin 63

Romanticism 9, 18, 50 64, 98, 101, 107, 110, 111, 125, 137, 138, 139, 140

Ruskin 49, 52-53

Saint-Simon 77

Sainte-Beuve 40

Saussure 15

Schönberg 11

Schopenhauer 58

science 9, 13, 14, 15, 16, 20, 23, 24, 25, 27, 28, 29, 30, 31, 32, 33, 34, 35, 36, 37, 39, 40, 41, 43, 44, 45, 46, 47, 49, 50, 53, 54, 56, 61, 63, 69, 71, 84, 85, 100, 104, 115, 118, 124, 125, 138, 140, 143, 145

Searle 132

sensation/sense impression 27, 30, 38, 55, 58, 67, 102, 103, 104, 112, 118, 124, 127, 132, 134, 137

sentence 112-113

Shakespeare 40

Shelley 95

simile 56, 58, 112

Sinclair, May 20

sisterhood of the arts 50, 63, 79

socialism 83, 98

sociology 25, 29, 30, 143

Some Imagist Poets 12, 18
Sorel 89, 98
soul 90, 100, 102, 107
Spencer 28-30, 37, 39, 42, 43, 44, 45, 143
stasis 30, 70, 73, 85, 89, 94, 96, 127, 128, 144, 147
The Statesman 77
Stuart Mill 25, 30, 31, 33, 35, 37, 38, 39, 40
style 55, 57, 71, 110, 113
sublime 15
Swinburne 53, 92
symbol 20, 45, 50, 65, 96, 102, 132
symbolism 18, 49, 63, 64-65, 76, 134
Symons 13, 64
synaesthesia 79, 134

Taine 13, 33-36, 37, 38, 40, 42, 44, 45, 46, 47, 95, 117
Tennyson 9, 21, 22
The Townsman 12
truth 14, 23, 26, 29, 32, 36, 37, 40, 41, 43, 45, 49, 54, 55, 62, 69, 72, 74, 82, 84, 88, 96, 100, 101, 115, 125, 143, 144, 145
Tschaikovsky 63
Turner 52, 107

Valéry 145
values 88-89
vers libéré 68, 76
vers libre/free verse 17, 53, 59, 68, 74-78, 109, 110, 111, 139, 141
Victorial poetry 9, 13, 92, 100, 101, 140, 141
vision 92, 101, 104, 105, 132
vital art 87, 89, 93-95
vocabulary 58, 129-131, 134, 135
Vortex 18, 21, 24

Wagner 68
Wheelwright 61
Whistler 14, 109
Whitman 74
Wilkinson, Marguerite 18, 78
Wittgenstein 16, 62, 67-68, 111, 113, 132
Wordsworth 55, 96, 101, 105

Worringer 72-73, 74

Yeats 80, 96, 102, 141
The Yellow Book 13

Zola 103, 107

NOTES

CHAPTER ONE. IMAGISM

NAME. ORIGIN MEMBERS
1. *Kraus Reprint Corporation New York 1962 vol. II,* pp. 65 et seq.
2. Vol. II, p.70
3. Vol. II, p. 72
4. Vol. II, p. 71
5. *Canzoni and Ripostes,* p. 134
6. pp. 122-123
7. Kenner, *The Pound Era,* p. 174
8. Coffman, *Imagism,* p. 122
9. Kenner, *The Poetry of Ezra Pound,* Appendix I, pp. 307-308
10. *Blasting and Bombardiering,* p. 106
11. *Life for Life's Sake,* p. 101

A NEW NOTE
12. ibid.
13. Lester, *Journey through…,* pp. 6-7
14. Grant, *Harold Monro,* p. 41
15. Farmer, *Le mouvement…,* p. 279
16. Burdett, *The Beardsley Period,* pp. 202 et seq.
17. *Le mouvement…,* p. 386
18. Kenner, *The Pound Era,* p. 152
19. Wingfield-Stratford, *The Victorian Sunset,* p. 112

THE WORLD AND THE POET
20. Doing, *Things…,* p. 5

LANGUAGE
21. Abrams, *Doing Things…,* p. 16
22. Holbrook Jackson, *The 1890s,* p. 136
23. Pound, *Gaudier-Brzeska,* p. 88
24. Grant, *Harold Monro,* p. 31
25. Vol. I, p. 272

26. Kenner, *The Pound Era,* p. 186
27. Kenner, op. cit., p. 230

FORM
28. Farmer, *Le mouvement…*, p. 386
29. Grant, *Harold Monroe*, p. 47
30. ibid.

THE IMAGIST PRINCIPLES
31. p. 241
32. p. 242
33. p. 246
34. p. 243
35. pp. 215-216
36. *New Voices*, p. 87
37. *Gaudier-Brzeska*, p. 114
38. p. 45
39. his italics; *Gaudier-Brzeska*, p. 86
40. ibid.
41. *Gaudier-Brzeska*, pp 86-87
42. Grant, *Harold Monroe*, p. 83

IMAGIST CRITICISME OF IMAGISM
43. *Imagist Anthology 1916*, p. 175
44. op.cit., p. 176
45. *Gaudier-Brzeska*, p. 42
46. Hough, *Image and Experience*, pp. 15-16
47. Coffman, *Imagism…*, p. 160
48. *Tendencies…*, p.243
49. *Image and Experience*, p. 13
50. Coffman, *Imagism…*, p. 12
51. vol. II, pp 65 et seq.
52. vol. I, p. 78
53. vol. I, p. 89
54. *The New Poetic…*, p. 99
55. *Tendencies…*, p. 279
56. ibid.
57. *Imagism…*, p. 23
58. *Edwardian Occasions*, pp. 125-126
59. Starkie, *From Gautier…*, p. 161

Vorticism
60. *Blast*, p. 154
61. op.cit., p.120

CHAPTER TWO. THE LATE 19th CENTURY SCIENTIFIC MODEL

Lord Kelvin
1. Thompson, *The Life…*, p. 1154
2. op. cit., p. 247
3. op. cit., p.248
4. op. cit., p. 247
5. op. cit., p. 437
6. op. cit., p. 806
7. op. cit., p. 517
8. op. cit., p. 1157

Reality
9. Culler, *On Deconstruction…*, p. 153

CHAPTER THREE. THE PERVASIVENESS OF THE MODEL

Ernst Mach
1. p. 15
2. ibid.
3. Blackmore, *Ernst Mach*, p. 10
4. *Leitgedanken*, p. 4
5. Blackmore, op. cit., p. 116
6. Blackmore, op. cit., p. 79
7. Blackmore, op. cit., pp. 89-90
8. Blackmore, op. cit., p. 116
9. Blackmore, op. cit., p. 115
10. Blackmore, op. cit., p. 124
11. Blackmore, op. cit., pp. 154-159

Herbert Spencer
12. p. 13
13. p. 18
14. pp. 14-15

15. p. 64
16. p. 60
17. p. 405
18. p. 402
19. p. 409
20. p. 316
21. p. 170
22. ibid.
23. p. 217
24. p. 218
25. p. 293
26. p. 257
27. p. 262
28. p. 373
29. p. 413

AUGUST COMTE
30. Mill, *August Comte...*, p. 153
31. op. cit., p. 155
32. op. cit., p. 15
33. Deherne, *Pensées...*, p. 31
34. Deherne, op. cit., p. 3
35. Deherne, op. cit., p. 95
36. Deherne, op. cit., p.43
37. Deherne, op. cit., p. 17
38. Deherne, op. cit., p. 9
39. Deherne, op. cit., p. 10
40. Deherne, op. cit., p. 29
41. Mill, op. cit., p. 83
42. Mill, op. cit., p.51
43. Deherne, op. cit., p. 9
44. Deherne, op. cit., p. 99
45. Deherne, op. cit., p. 95
46. Mill, op. cit., p. 149
47. Mill, op. cit., p. 143
48. Deherne, op. cit., p. 11
49. Deherne, op. cit., p. 68
50. Mill, op. cit., p. 44
51. Deherne, op. cit., p.23
52. Deherne, op. cit., p. 3

53. Deherne, op., cit. p. 101
54. Deherne, op., cit. p. 18
55. Mill, op. cit., p. 175
56. ibid.
57. Mill, op. cit., p. 176
58. Mill, op. cit., p. 169
59. Mill, op. cit., p. 138
60. Deherne, op. cit., p. 96
61. Mill, op. cit., p. 181

HIPPOLYTE TAINE
62. pp. 19-20
63. p. 81
64. Cresson, *Hippolyte Taine...*, p. 9
65. Cresson, op. cit., p. 24
66. Cresson, op. cit., p. 90
67. Cresson, op. cit., p. 105
68. *De l'Intelligence, Livre 1er chap. 1er.* Cresson, op. cit., p. 126
69. Cresson, op. cit., pp 56-57
70. Nordmann, *Taine...*, p. 123
71. Nordmann, op. cit., p. 262
72. Cresson, op. cit., p. 28
73. Cresson, op. cit., pp. 136-137
74. Cresson, op. cit., p. 29
75. Cresson, op. cit., p. 14
76. Cresson, op. cit., p. 41
77. Cresson, op. cit., p. 35
78. Nordmann, op. cit., p. 106
79. *Philosophie...*, p. 395
80. Nordmann, op. cit., p.201
81. Nordmann, op. cit., p. 252
82. Nordmann, op. cit., p. 129
83. *Philosophie...*, p. 440

CHAPTER FOUR. POSITIVISM AND ITS LIMITATIONS

POSITIVISM
1. Nordmann, *Taine...*, p. 35
2. *Philosophie...*, p. 385

3. *Pensées…*, p. 357
4. p. 14
5. Nordmann, op. cit., p 54
6. *Pensées*, p. 33
7. Mill, *Comte…*, p. 6
8. Mill, op. cit., p. 15
9. Mach, *Leitgedanken*, p. 28
10. p. 10
11. Mill. op. cit., p. 451
12. Mill. op. cit., p. 100
13. *First Principles*, p. 180

LIMITATIONS
14. Mill, *Comte…*, p. 63
15. *Pensées*, p. 79
16. Nordmann, *Taine…*, p. 264
17. Nordmann, op. cit., p. 331

THE SCIENTISTS
18. Comte, *Pensées*, p. 24
19. Blackmore, *Ernst Mach…*, p. XVII
20. *Leitgedanken*, p. 18
21. Blackmore, op. cit., p. 222
22. Blackmore, op. cit., p. 115
23. Blackmore, op. cit., p. 226
24. *Draft Foreword to the Russian Translation of Die Analyse der Empfindungen.* Blackmore, op. cit., p. 115
25. Blackmore, op. cit., p. 226
26. Blackmore, op. cit., p. 225
27. *Die Analyse der Empfikdungen*, p.236
28. Blackmore, op. cit., p. 225
29. Blackmore, op. cit., pp. 227-228
30. Thompson, *The Life of William Thomson*, p. 1091
31. Thompson, op. cit., p. 1092
32. Thompson, op. cit., p. 1147

THE PHILOSOPHERS
33. *First Principles*, p. 77
34. op. cit., p. 183
35. *Pensées*, p. 4

36. Mill, *Comte…*, p.184
37. Mill, op. cit. p., 178
38. *Pensées,* p. 28
39. *Pensées,* p. 169
40. *First Principles,* p. 104
41. *First Principles,* p. 91
42. *First Principles,* p. 392
43. Mill, op. cit., p. 62
44. Mill, op. cit., p. 59
45. *Pensées,* p. 59
46. Mill, op. cit., p. 62
47. *First Principles,* p. 446
48. *First Principles,* p. 224
49. *Pensées,* p. 5
50. *First Principles,* p. 69
51. *First Principles,* pp. 37-42
52. *First Principles,* p. 125
53. Mill, *Comte…*, p. 6
54. *First Principles,* p. 27
55. *Pensées,* pp. 12-13
56. *First Principles,* p. 24
57. *First Principles,* p. 428
58. Cresson, *Hippolyte Taine…*, p. 116
59. *First Principles,* p. 34
60. *First Principles,* p. 63
61. Nordmann, *Taine…*, p. 333
62. *Pensées,* p. 98
63. *First Principles,* p. 65
64. *First Principles,* p. 50
65. *First Principles,* p. 182
66. *First Principles,* p. 15
67. *First Principles,* p. 50
68. *Pensées,* p. 240
69. *Pensées,* p. 249
70. Cresson, *Hippolyte Taine…*, p. 11
71. Taine, *Philosophie…*, p. 96
72. Taine, *Philosophie…*, p. 78

CHAPTER FIVE. COUNTERCURRENTS

1. Burdett, *The Beardsley Period*, p. 96

L'ART POUR L'ART
2. Cassagne, *La théorie...*, p. 117
3. Cassagne, *La théorie...*, p. 263
4. Cassagne, op. cit., p. 112

THEODOR LIPPS
5. *Raumästetik...*, pp. 35-36
6. *Grundlegung der Astetik,* vol. II, pp. 62 et seq.

JOHN RUSKIN
7. *Sesame and Lilies* (1933), p. 157
8. Quenel, *John Ruskin*, p. 29
9. Quenell, op. cit., p. 20

FRENCH INFLUENCE
10. *Mélanges posthumes,* p. 115

MIMESIS
11. Abrams, *Doing Things...*, p. 22
12. Abrams, op. cit., p. 183

CREATION. RIBOT
13. *Essai...*, p. 27
14. op. cit., p. 37
15. op. cit., p. 105

GOURMONT
16. Vol. I, pp. 101-103
17. Vol. II, p. 169
18. *Le problème du style*, p. 9
19. op. cit., p. 12
20. op. cit., p. 35
21. op. cit., p. 47
22. op. cit., p. 31
23. op. cit., p. 122
24. *Premiers poèmes. Domaine de fée X*

25. ibid.
26. *Le problème du style,* p. 100

LAFORGUE
27. *Mélanges posthumes,* p. 43
28. op. cit., pp. 129-130
29. op. cit., pp. 133 et seq.
30. op. cit., p. 136
31. *Premiers poèmes. Domaine de fée X*
32. *Premiers poèmes X. La rue comme un regret*
33. *Premiers poèmes. Domaine de fée X*
34. *Premiers poèmes Chanson d'amant XVIII*
35. *Premiers poèmes. Domaine de fée XI*

CHAPTER SIX. BREAKTHROUGH OF THE ANTI-POSITIVISTS

PLANCK
1. Blackmore, *Ernst Mach,* p. 130
2. Blackmore, op. cit., p. 131
3. Blackmore, op. cit., p. 128
4. Blackmore, op. cit., p. 131
5. *Metaphor and Reality,* p. 173

EINSTEIN
6. p. 27

THE HUMANITIES
7. *Make it new,* p. 17

SYMBOLISM
8. Wilson, *Axel's Castle,* pp. 12 et seq.
9. Symons, *The Symbolist Movement…,* p. 3
10. Symons, op. cit., p. 138
11. Lester, *Journey through…,* p. 117
12. Starkie, *From Gautier…,* p. 95
13. Symons, op. cit., p. 146
14. Kenner, *The Poetry of Ezra Pound,* p. 98
15. Jules Lemaître, *Les Contemporains,* vol. II, p. 119

CHAPTER SEVEN. INDEBTEDNESS

BERGSON
1. *Evoluition créatrice*, p. 57
2. op. cit., p. 290
3. op. cit., p. 324
4. *Matière et Mémoire*, p. 230
5. *Matière et Mémoire*, p. 7
6. *Matière et Mémoire*, p. IV
7. ibid.

BERGSON AND HULME
8. Coffman, *Imagism…*, pp. 54-55

WORRINGER
9. *Abstraktion und Einfühlung* (transl. Bullock), p. VII
10. op. cit., p. 6
11. op. cit., p.11
12. op. cit., p. 29
13. op. cit., p. 44
14. op. cit., p. 52
15. op. cit., p. 55
16. op. cit., p. 20
17. Jones, *The Life and Opinions…*, p. 210

VERS LIBRE
18. Starkie, *From Gautier…*, pp. 98-99
19. Kahn, *Premiers poèmes*, p. 17
20. Kahn, op. cit., p. 16
21. Kahn, op. cit., p. 23
22. Kahn, op. cit., p. 9
23. Kahn, op. cit., pp. 22-23
24. Kahn, op. cit., p. 26
25. Kahn, op. cit., p. 28
26. Kahn, *Le vers libre*, p. 37
27. Kahn, *Premiers poèmes*, p. 33
28. Kahn, *Le vers libre*, p. 29
29. Kahn, *Premiers poèmes*, p. 33
30. Kahn, *Premiers poèmes*, p. 28
31. Kahn, *Premiers poèmes*, p. 34

32. Kahn, *Le vers libre,* p. 29
33. Kahn, *Le vers libre,* p. 31
34. Kahn, *Le vers libre,* p. 32
35. Kahn, *Le vers libre,* p. 37
36. ibid.
37. ibid.
38. Kahn, *Le vers libre,* p. 37
39. Kahn, *Le vers libre,* p. 37
40. ibid.
41. *Premiers poèmes,* p. 17
42. *Le problème du style,* p. 165
43. February 16, 1914, vol. I, p. 75
44. September 15, 1914, vol. I, pp. 351-352
45. p. 262
46. p. 264
47. ibid.
48. p. 263
49. *The Egoist,* July 1917, vol. IV, pp. 90-91
50. *New Voices,* p. 37
51. *Hughes Imagism…,* p. 73
52. *Premiers poèmes,* p. 32
53. *The History of Imagism. The Egoist,* May 1, 1915
54. *Preface to the collection of poetry called Irradiations – TRUE and Spray,* April 1915
55. Lowell, *Modern American Poetry,* pp. 298-299
56. Lowell, op. cit., p. 299
57. Hough, *Imagism…,* p. 89
58. Hough, op. cit., p. 90

Dance
59. pp. 143-144
60. *Journey through…,* pp. 147-148
61. *Further Speculations,* p. 99
62. *Further Speculations,* p. 91
63. *Further Speculations,* p. 96
64. *Further Speculations,* p. 90
65. *Further Speculations,* pp. 139-140
66. *Further Speculations,* p. 82

CHAPTER EIGHT. HULME'S PHILOSOPHY

Introduction
1. *Speculations,* p. 227
2. op. cit., pp. 93-94

Absolutes
3. *The Religious Attitude. Speculations,* p. 68
4. *Speculations,* p. 9
5. Roberts, *T.E.Hulme,* p. 134
6. *Speculations,* p. 250
7. *Speculations,* p. 58
8. *Speculations,* p. 16
9. *Speculations.* p. 21
10. *A Critique of Satisfaction. Speculations,* p. 22
11. *Speculations,* p. 53

Hulme and Science
12. *A Critique of Satisfaciton. Speculations,* p. 21
13. Roberts, *T.E.Hulme,* p. 138

Bergson
14. Nott, *The Emperor's Clothes,* p. 98

Dichotomies
15. *Speculations,* p. 146
16. op. cit., p. 58

Intuition versus Intellect
17. *Speculations,* p. 182
18. Nott, *The Emperor's Clothes,* p. 2
19. *Speculations,* p. 179
20. *Speculations,* p. 188
21. *Speculations,* p. 146
22. *Speculations,* p. 174
23. *Speculations,* p. 189

Manifolds
24. *Speculations,* p. 177
25. op. cit., p. 194

26. op. cit., p. 181
27. op. cit., p. 201
28. op. cit., p. 204

Humanism and Religion
29. *Speculations,* p. 47
30. op. cit., p. 8
31. op. cit., p. 100
32. op. cit., p. 59
33. op. cit., p. 35

Values
34. *Speculations,* p. 239

Conclusion
35. *Speculations,* p. 71
36. op. cit., p. 3
37. op. cit., p. 226
38. op. cit., p. 175
39. Roberts, *T.E.Hulme,* p. 121
40. *Speculations,* pp. 50-52
41. Roberts, *T.E.Hulme,* pp. 86-87
42. Nott, *The Emperor's Clothes,* p. 75
43. *Speculations,* p. 227
44. *Speculations,* p. 250
45. *Speculations,* p. 241

CHAPTER NINE. HULME'S AESTHETICS

Introduction
1. *Polite Essays,* p. 9
2. Jones, *The Life…of T.E.Hulme,* p. 101

The Purpose of Art
3. *Further Speculations,* p. 97
4. Roberts, *T.E.Hulme,* p. 163
5. *Further Speculations,* p. 97
6. *Speculations,* p. 141
7. *Further Speculations,* p. 92

8. ibid.
9. *Further Speculations*, p. 82
10. *Further Speculations*, p. 128
11. *Further Speculations*, p. 97
12. ibid.
13. ibid.
14. *Speculations*, pp. 150-151

FORM
15. *Further Speculations*, p. 116
16. op. cit., pp. 139-140

GEOMETRIC VERSUS VITAL ART
17. *Speculations*, p. 78
18. op. cit., p. 107
19. ibid.
20. op. cit., p. 86
21. op. cit., p. 84
22. Jones, *The Life…of T.E.Hulme*, p. 17
23. Jones, p. 20
24. *Speculations*, p. 128
25. *Speculations*, p. 124
26. *Speculations*, p. 78
27. *Further Speculations*, p. 125

CLASSICAL VERSUS ROMANTIC
28. Nordmann, *Taine*, p. 219
29. *Speculations*, p. 10
30. *Speculations*, p.116
31. *Speculations*, p. 17
32. *Speculations*, p. 118
33. ibid.
34. *Speculations*, p.120

BEAUTY
35. *Speculations*, p. 136
36. *Further Speculations*, p. 97
37. *Further Speculations*, p. 98
38. *Further Speculations*, p. 93
39. *Further Speculations*, p. 98

40. *Further Speculations,* p. 99
41. ibid.
42. *Further Speculations,* p. 97
43. *Further Speculations,* p. 90

CREATION
44. *Speculations,* p. 147
45. op. cit., p. 151
46. op. cit., p. 149
47. op. cit., p. 152

HULME AND POLITICS
48. *Reflections on Violence. Speculations,* pp. 252 et seq.
49. *Speculations,* pp. 113-114
50. op. cit., pp. 259-260
51. op. cit., p.252
52. op. cit., p. 249

CHAPTER TEN. HULME'S LITERARY THEORIES

INTRODUCTION
1. p. 238
2. *Further Speculations,* p. 98
3. op. cit., p. 91
4. Hughes, *Imagism…,* p. 51
5. *Further Speculations,* p. 87
6. *Further Speculations,* p. 85
7. *Further Speculations,* p. 95
8. *Further Speculations,* p. 67
9. *Further Speculations,* p.74
10. *Further Speculations,* p. 75
11. *Further Speculations,* p. 67
12. *Further Speculations,* p. 75

SCIENCE AND POETRY
13. *Further Speculations,* p. 93
14. op. cit., p 76
15. op. cit., p. 75
16. op. cit., p. 84

The Poet
17. *Further Speculations*, p. 83
18. op. cit., p. 94
19. op. cit., p. 93
20. op. cit., p 94
21. op. cit., p. 85
22. op. cit., pp. 99-100
23. op. cit., p. 100
24. op. cit., p. 69
25. op. cit., p. 78
26. op. cit., p. 94

Literature and its Raw Materials
27. *Further Speculations*, p. 88
28. ibid.
29. op. cit., p. 85
30. op. cit., p. 99
31. op. cit., p. 82
32. op. cit., p. 99
33. op. cit., p. 92

The Creative Process
34. Starkie, *From Gautier…*, p. 35
35. *Further Speculations*, p. 84
36. *Further Speculations*, p. 83
37. *Further Speculations*, p. 78
38. *Further Speculations*, p. 82
39. *Further Speculations*, p. 84
40. *Further Speculations*, p. 94
41. *Speculations*, p. 136
42. *Further Speculations*, p. 146
43. *Speculations*, p. 137
44. *Further Speculations*, p. 80
45. *Speculations*, p. 133
46. *Further Speculations*, p. 91
47. *Further Speculations*, p. 94
48. ibid.
49. *Further Speculations*, p. 95
50. *Further Speculations*, p. 91
51. *Further Speculations*, p. 92

52. *Further Speculations*, p. 99
53. *Further Speculations*, p. 100

FANCY AND IMAGINATION
54. *Speculations*, pp. 116 et seq.
55. Krieger, *The New Apologists*, p. 33
56. *Speculations*, p. 138
57. *Speculations*, p. 134
58. ibid.
59. *Speculations*, p. 138

THE SUBJECT
60. Roberts, *T.E.Hulme*, p. 66
61. *Further Speculations*, p. 71
62. *Speculations*, p. 97

MIMESIS
63. *Further Speculations*, p. 98
64. op. cit., p. 99
65. op. cit., p. 98
66. *Speculations*, p. 98
67. *Further Speculations*, p. 98
68. *Further Speculations*, p. 97
69. *Further Speculations*, p. 86

FORM
70. *Further Speculations* p. 71
71. op. cit., p. 98
72. op. cit., p. 71
73. op. cit., p. 76
74. op. cit., p. 68
75. ibid.
76. op. cit., p. 68
77. op. cit., p. 69
78. op. cit., p. 70
79. op. cit., p. 72
80. ibid.
81. op. cit., p. 70
82. op. cit., p. 68
83. op. cit., p. 73
84. op. cit., p. 74

85. op. cit., p. 69
86. ibid.
87. op. cit., p. 73
88. op. cit., p. 75
89. op. cit., p. 71
90. op. cit., p. 73
91. ibid.
92. op. cit., p. 70
93. op. cit., p. 75
94. op. cit., p. 73
95. op. cit., p. 78
96. op. cit., p.69

LANGUAGE
97. *Speculations*, p. 132
98. *Further Speculations*, p. 83
99. *Further Speculations*, p. 85
100. *Philosophy of Rhetoric*, Lecture IV
101. *Further Speculations*, p. 84
102. *Further Speculations*, p. 8
103. *Further Speculations*, p. 83
104. *Doing Things...*, p. 355
105. *Further Speculations*, p. 86
106. *Speculations*, p. 244
107. *Further Speculations*, p. 79
108. *Further Speculations*, p. 13
109. *Further Speculations*, p. 86
110. *Further Speculations*, p. 88
111. *Further Speculations*, p. 87
112. *Further Speculations*, p. 88
113. *Further Speculations*, p. 74
114. *Further Speculations*, p. 83
115. ibid.

CINDERS AND COUNTERS
116. *Further Speculations*, p. 78
117. *Speculations*, pp. 134-135
118. *Speculations*, p. 152
119. *Further Speculations*, pp. 74-75
120. *Further Speculations*, p. 85

121. *Further Speculations*, p. 84
122. *Further Speculations*, p. 78
123. ibid.
124. *Further Speculations*, p. 79
125. ibid.
126. *Further Speculations*, p. 74
127. *Further Speculations*, p. 85
128. *Further Speculations*, p. 94
129. p. 283
130. *Speculations*, p. 243
131. *Speculations*, p. 220
132. *Further Speculations*, p. 94
133. *Speculations*, p. 243
134. *Speculations*, p. 224
135. *Speculations*, p. 231
136. *Speculations*, p. 222
137. *Further Speculations*, p. 80
138. *Speculations*, p. 224
139. *Further Speculations*, p. 97

THE FUNCTION OF THE IMAGE.
140. transl. Baron London 1906, p. 12
141. Nordmann, *Taine*, p. 330
142. *Further Speculations*, p. 82
143. *Further Speculations*, p. 87
144. *Further Speculations*, p. 88
145. *Further Speculations*, p. 90
146. *Further Speculations*, p. 96

THE READER
147. *Further Speculations*, p. 88
148. *Speculations*, p. 153

THE OBJECTIVE CORRELATIVE
149. *Further Speculations*, p. 82
150. *Speculations*, p. 168
151. Bodelsen, *T.S.Eliot's Four Quartets*, p. 3
152. *Speculations*, p. 168
153. *The New Apologists*, pp. 49-50
154. Matthiesen, *The Achievement of T.S.Eliot*, p. 64

CHAPTER ELEVEN. HULME'S POEMS

INTRODUCTION
1. Jones, *The Life...of T.E.Hulme*, pp. 55-56

COMPOSITION
2. Hynes, *Edwardian Occasions*, p. 38

FORM
3. Coffman, *Imagism...*, p. 12

IMAGES
4. Black, *A Companion...*, p. 159
5. op. cit., p. 160
6. *Poetics*, p. 45
7. Nowottny, *The Language Poets Use*, p. 57
8. *Intentionality...*, p. 146
9. *Models and Metaphors*, p. 39
10. Olsen, *Elements of Textual Analysis*, pp. 89-90

CHAPTER TWELVE. HULME CRITICISM

1. p. 17
2. pp. 226-228
3. p. 207
4. p. 66
5. p. 154
6. p. 68
7. p. 37
8. p. 35
9. pp. 54 et seq.
10. p. 13
11. p. X
12. p. XV
13. p. XIV
14. p. IX
15. p. XV
16. p. XIX
17. p. XV

18. p. 51
19. pp. 54-56
20. p. 73
21. p. 74
22. p. 12
23. p. 24
24. p. 75
25. p. 83
26. p. 28
27. p. 34
28. p. 70
29. p. 156
30. ibid.
31. p. 15

CONCLUSION

HULME
1. *Further Speculations,* p. 20
2. op. cit., p. 12
3. op. cit., p. 15
4. Hough, *Image and Experience…,* p. 16

THE LEGACY. ELIOT
5. Coffman, *Imagism…,* pp. 218-220
6. *Tradition and the Individual Talent. Selected Essays,* p. 21
7. Stead, *The New Poetic,* p. 122
8. pp. 231-232

FINAL REMARKS
9. *Edwardian Occasions,* pp. 125-126
10. Culler, *On Deconstruction…,* p. 22